Multicultural Literacies

Studies in the
Postmodern Theory of Education

Joe L. Kincheloe and Shirley R. Steinberg
General Editors

Vol. 45

PETER LANG
New York • Washington, D.C./Baltimore
Bern • Frankfurt am Main • Berlin • Vienna • Paris

Patrick L. Courts

Multicultural Literacies

Dialect, Discourse, and Diversity

PETER LANG
New York • Washington, D.C./Baltimore
Bern • Frankfurt am Main • Berlin • Vienna • Paris

Library of Congress Cataloging-in-Publication Data

Courts, Patrick L.
Multicultural literacies: dialect, discourse, and diversity/
Patrick L. Courts.
p. cm. —(Counterpoints: vol. 45)
Includes bibliographical references and index.
1. Language arts—United States. 2. Literacy—Social aspects—United States.
3. Postmodernism and education—United States. 4. Critical Pedagogy—
United States. 5. Language experience approach in education—United States.
6. Multicultural education—United States. 7. Sociolinguistics.
I. Title. II. Series: Counterpoints (New York, NY); vol. 45.
LB1576.C747 302.2'244—dc20 95-42973
ISBN 0-8204-3675-5
ISSN 1058-1634

Die Deutsche Bibliothek-CIP-Einheitsaufnahme

Courts, Patrick L.:
Multicultural literacies: dialect, discourse, and diversity/
Patrick L. Courts. – New York; Washington, D.C./Baltimore; Bern;
Frankfurt am Main; Berlin; Vienna; Paris: Lang.
(Counterpoints; Vol. 45)
ISBN 0-8204-3675-5
NE: GT

Cover design by James F. Brisson.

The paper in this book meets the guidelines for permanence and durability
of the Committee on Production Guidelines for Book Longevity
of the Council of Library Resources.

Printed in the United States of America.

Acknowledgments

I wish to express my gratitude to the following people who helped me in the writing and revising of this book:

Minda Rae Amiran, whose painstaking editorial comments and critical questioning made this book much better than it might have been;

Karen Mills-Courts, one of the best teachers I know, whose careful and extensive critical commentary and support were essential throughout the entire writing process;

Mike Conley, an old friend, whose general knowledge of linguistics and specific knowledge of the Chinese and Japanese languages and cultures helped me so much in the early stages of the book and whose editorial feedback assisted me in the final stages;

Penny Deakin, who, as always, bothered to give the manuscript a careful reading and insightful feedback and who joined me in discussions about discourse systems before either of us knew exactly what we were discussing;

Tom Malinowski, who shared his own stories about and experiences with Native Americans, who provided me with important articles to read, and even more important, good talk;

Vai Ramanathan-Abbott, who showered me with articles and books to help me with my initial stages of research;

The many students who have, through class discussion and their own writing, forced me to clarify my own thinking on the complex issues in the book;

Donaldo Macedo, James Gee, Peter McLaren, who encouraged the entire project;

And especially, Shirley Steinberg and Joe Kincheloe who agreed to publish the book as part of their Counterpoints series.

Of course, none of these people is responsible for the book's weaknesses, but many of them are directly responsible for its strengths.

Series Editor's Preface

Literacy seems to be the word *du jour* in education. Inserting it within every catch phrase, there has been an attempt to acknowledge the need to "be literate." However, as we enter the twenty-first century, Americans are entering with the lowest literacy rate in the first world. The New Right blames the immigration "problem" and the influx of non-English speaking people. Next on the blame list are the "people of color," Charles Murray's and Richard Herrnstein's *Bell Curve* answer to why there is a lack of literacy. Colleges of education pound this word, literacy, into their strategic planning sessions and new curriculums—yet, defined through narrow, modernistic phrases, literacy becomes synonymous with maintaining a western canon, marginalizing non-dominant culture peoples and reinforcing an air of illiteracy.

As educators we are constantly bombarded with the anti-multiculturalist, the anti-diversity colleagues who scream that this "new" curriculum is usurping all that we have held dear. As the newly marginalized, these curriculum fascists hold the bastions of teacher education hostage to ignorance and anti-intellectualism.

Patrick Courts sees this imprisonment of literacy curriculum. Considering social justice as first and foremost, Courts includes literacy through culture and politics as essential as learning the alphabet. No longer minimizing literacy as a way "to get by" in society, he is able to enliven the discourse with acknowledging that in order to succeed in this world, our students must be extra-literate, in that they know the discourse of the dominant culture and know the discourse in which they chose to live and thrive. While not marginalizing one's own positionality, Courts illustrates that as long as we live within hegemonic, paranoid culture, we will have to educate our students to be fluent in as many "languages" as it takes for them to succeed.

Teachers of literacy spend time trying to impose "standards" upon students without acknowledging or studying the discourse in which students are comfortable. This cultural illiteracy of students perpetuates the inability of teachers to work with students. I am reminded of a professor in a college of education who purported to teach a critical literacy for teachers, but would not acknowledge the use of a "Zine" in publication as authentic text—teachers who constantly refer to student dialect as "street language" or "inappropriate" are perpetuating an elitism that negates any personal experience or voice. There is an implication that to incorporate a student's lived curriculum is to simplify scholarship. The use of teen music or culture somehow minimalizes language. Back to the "only if it hurts" curriculum of the New Right. Learning shouldn't be interesting or fun, it should be administered as a bitter medicine—as a cure. Courts understands the importance of individual voice, he also understands the importance of succeeding within a dominant culture. As teachers we must learn to teach two curriculums for success, curriculums in which students can move in and out of with comfort and self-esteem.

Shirley R. Steinberg
Adelphi University

Joe L. Kincheloe
Penn State University

For Karen,
who sees more than most in a leaf of grass,
who generously shares the vision.

Contents

Author's Introduction

Over the past 26 years, especially in my own teaching of a course called "Language, Literacy, and Learning Theory" and literature courses focusing on literary works across a broad range of cultures, I have become increasingly aware of how powerfully my students are affected by their own discovery of sociolinguistic issues. Indeed, it has been their excited responses and confusions surrounding issues of dialect and discourse as they apply their new knowledge to the teaching of literacy that primarily motivates my writing.

This book traverses some mightily troubled waters and explores issues that lead many people into highly emotional positions. Just the suggestion that non-dominant dialects of English are as valid, effective, and worthy as the dominant dialect (Standard English) is often enough to set the self-ordained guardians of language and culture into states of apoplexy. Others may see the examination of primary discourse systems as a crazed, politically-correct argument for eliminating the use of "clear organization and logic" in the development of well-written essays: they may well argue that, just because some Chinese, or Chicana(o)s, or African Americans think, speak, and develop arguments and narratives counter to the rules of "essayist literacy," this is no reason to make excuses for them. They can learn to talk, write, and think correctly just like the rest of us. Some readers may accept the validity of non-dominant discourse systems but will object that, because of sociolinguistic (and racial/ethnic) bias, we must force the non-dominant speakers/writers to acquire the dominant discourse or they will be locked out of the dominant society (as though they are not already locked out of the dominant society). Some may even choose to misread the book and decide that it is a veiled attempt to keep people locked inside their non-domi-

nant discourse systems: by pretending to respect and admire
non-dominant discourse systems, we will insure that minorities will never have access to the dominant culture. These last
two groups will have missed the central point of the book: It is
our job as teachers of literacy to provide learners the *knowledge and opportunity to choose and control* their discourses and to
know when they are being discriminated against because of their
uses of non-dominant dialects/discourses. From my point of
view, it would be an unethical teacher who wanted to keep any
learners locked inside their primary discourses. This book,
then, is not only about the validity of non-dominant discourse
systems and encouraging students to become facile, powerful
users of their primary discourse systems: it is about exploring
ways in which all learners can acquire the secondary discourse
systems that they need to acquire in order to move beyond the
isolation of their various geographical and cultural ghettoes,
should they choose to make such a move. It is about what teachers must know and do in order to right the wrongs that are
done to so many people whose culture and language differ
from that of the powerful, dominant institutions and individuals who "make the rules."

I hope to make at least one thing clear from the outset: In
this book I propose that we honor and respect all non-dominant dialect and discourse systems. But I also argue that, by
doing so, schools can offer students the opportunity to attain
higher degrees of literacy. Most important, I argue that regardless of the dominance or non-dominance of a given discourse system, all of us need to know more about our own and
others' discourse systems in order to:

1. Communicate better and more respectfully with others;
2. Have the opportunity to acquire various secondary Discourse systems that will provide us with the opportunity
   to move in and about communities different from the ones
   we grow up in; and
3. Improve the teaching of literacy in our schools.

Quite simply, by learning about and respecting our own and
others' discourse systems, militating against linguistic and cultural biases, and providing students an opportunity to become

knowledgeable, conscious users of their own and others' discourse systems, we can offer them the possibility to more fully and happily realize their own potentials. And one last point, the book is also about the genuine joy, the fun we can all have if we stop being so uptight about language "correctness" and begin to hear the voices and ideas of the peoples who enrich and comprise our society.

Chapter 1

Politeracies: Marginalizers and Those They Marginalize

The problems of the American of color are real. Ghettoes are growing larger, not smaller. Racism seems more entrenched than ever, a
condition that arises whenever there are larger economic problems.
And the gap between the rich and the poor continues to widen, the
rich needing the poor to keep whatever riches they have. And the
ghetto dwellers grow desperate and begin to believe less and less that
there is hope even for the next generation coming up. And crackheads
crack heads and zip guns become uzis and gangs take on corporate
quality. Crips, Inc. And Bloods, Inc. National gang networks with
corporate headquarters in Los Angeles. And their problems become
everyone's problems in one sense or another. Economic problems,
and the ways in which they shape our lives, hegemonically, place us
all—Americans—in the same postmodern boat. (Villanueva: 141–142)

[W]e argue for the necessity of developing a politics and a pedagogy
of voice as part of a theory of curriculum that opens up texts to a
wider range of meanings and interpretations, while simultaneously
constructing student experience as part of a broader discourse of critical citizenship and democracy. [W]e emphasize that teaching must be
seen as part of a larger curriculum project related to the construction
of political subjects and the formation of schools as democratic public spheres. We also develop the position that administrators and teachers need to . . . reject the cult of knowledge, expertise, and disembodied rationality that permeates the discourse of curriculum theory.
(Aronowitz and Giroux: 88–89)

This is a book about the acquisition and teaching of literacy
and Discourse systems. But perhaps, more so, it is a book about
those of us who are floating in Villanueva's "postmodern boat,"
particularly as that boat sails through our educational system.
It is a book about the kinds of oars, sails, navigational systems,
and perhaps good luck that we need to sail through the troubled

waters described by Villanueva. It is unquestionably a book about people of color, but since I know no colorless people, it is about all of us. It is also a book that accepts the challenge issued by Aronowitz and Giroux: by focusing on people as speakers and writers and hearers and readers—people as thinking *participants* in their education, this book examines teaching, particularly the teaching of literacy, as "part of a larger curriculum project related to the construction of political subjects and the formation of schools as democratic public spheres."

I begin with the quote from Villanueva because his book, *Bootstraps: From an American Academic of Color,* is an important mixture of scholarly comments about language and literacy in the United States and the educational/cultural experience that shape this specific Nuyorican as he moves toward capturing his own doctoral degree and becomes a member of academia. In many ways, much of this book is about the issue that Villanueva refers to when he discusses "racelessness . . . the decision to go it alone . . . most clearly marked linguistically, sometimes even by denying that one is choosing to learn to speak white English, by asserting that one is choosing to speak 'correct' English. A notion propagated by linguists who eschew the color or even the prestige of the dominant dialect labeling it as the value-free standard" (Villanueva: 40).

But before examining individual experiences, like Villanueva's, and especially before generalizing about or abstracting from those experiences in an attempt to suggest both a theory and a methodology for teaching literacy in our schools, the sociopolitical ground must be established. Thus, I also begin with the statement by Aronowitz and Giroux for several reasons, not the least of which is the fact that it indicates the kinds of tensions and oppositions that, too often silently and in disguise, permeate discussions of educational reform in the United States. To suggest that conservative educators and critical educators have engaged in a war of rhetoric is an understatement; the rhetoric of both sides often smacks of self-righteousness, and self-righteous rhetoric always needs to be examined. But it is equally important to note that the conservatives in this conflict pretty much own the media that report on American education, as well as owning the schools, controlling curricula, setting the "standards," and overseeing and regulating the monies that support education in the United States. I have seldom seen Giroux, Aronowitz, Freire, Peter McLaren, et al. mentioned in a newspaper or on the national television news.

Indeed, much that Giroux and Aronowitz say in this brief quotation, not to mention throughout their body of writings, is what various conservative spokespersons misrepresent and attack when making their arguments against the radical reforms so desperately needed in the American educational system. Highly influential conservatives who exercise considerable power when it comes to setting educational policy in this country—people like Diane Ravitch, William Bennett, Lynn Cheney, E. D. Hirsch, and the late Alan Bloom argue for things like "standards," "cultural literacy," "the classics," and they are emphatically in favor of "the cult of knowledge, expertise, and disembodied rationality that permeates the discourse of curriculum theory" (Macedo, 1994: 39). Their arguments often suggest that other reformers—those involved in liberatory or radical pedagogy—are somehow against standards, cultural literacy, and the classics. Conservative spokespersons often suggest that schools have become too "permissive," allowing students too much freedom to do whatever they choose as they willfully disregard authority. And I regularly see the Bennetts, et al. quoted in newspapers and on network news shows.

These conservative critics might, for example, suggest that opening up "texts to a wider range of meanings and interpretations, while simultaneously constructing student experience as part of a broader discourse of critical citizenship and democracy" is exactly the kind of educational philosophy that is ruining American schools and the students within them. The implementation of such a philosophy, they might argue, means that anything anyone thinks is acceptable and there is no right or wrong interpretation of any given text. This in turn, they argue, means that students are to be congratulated and praised for whatever they say or write and however they say it or write it. Furthermore, they might see the simultaneous construction of "student experience as part of a broader discourse of critical citizenship and democracy" as just another euphemism for replacing the wisdom and knowledge of educated adults for the silly and potentially dangerous egocentrism of youth.

Recently, for example, William Bennett, chair of NEH under President Reagan, attacked NEH summer workshops for teachers K–College—seminars and institutes he helped to create while chair. And what is the danger of these seminars and institutes? Bennett explains that the programs have been ruined by "political correctness": "'The books were being Marxized, feminized, deconstructed, and politicized. . . . High school teachers, far from being exposed to 'The best which has been thought and said in the world' (Matthew Arnold's phrase), were being indoctrinated in the prevailing dogmas of academia" (*Council Chronicle*, June 1995: 12). Indeed, conservatives like Bennett and his powerful, politically-connected allies would almost certainly view any rejection of "the cult of knowledge, expertise, and disembodied rationality that permeates the discourse of curriculum theory" as a wholesale overturning of the best that has been said and written by the sacred sages of various canons that have characterized school textbooks of the last 50 years (or 150 years, if we go back to Bennett's Matthew Arnold reference).

Of course, in making such an argument the conservative critics are careful to avoid exploring those who Aronowitz and Giroux refer to as members of the cult—and given that the Cheney's and Hirsch's are among the leaders of the cult, that is hardly surprising. Giroux and Aronowitz are not simplistically attacking knowledge and expertise; they are attacking the elitists—those who represent the power structure—who believe that it is up to them to decide what knowledge and what expertise most matter. People like Giroux, Aronowitz, and Macedo are attacking the people who, like Hirsch and his cohorts, believe they have the right and the responsibility (given by whom?) to decide "what every American needs to know"; they are criticizing the people who make considerable amounts of money first through being supported by NEH grants that allow them to write lists of what everyone needs to know and then to write something like *Dictionary of Cultural Literacy* (Hirsch, et al., 1987). It is not the knowledge and expertise they argue against, but the cult, the privatization of who it is who gets to decide who has *the right* knowledge and expertise.

And given the power of the conservative arguments, given the threats the conservatives see emanating from such dangerous reformers, I have had to take pause myself and wonder at the fact that I find so many of these "radical" ideas presented by people like Giroux, Aronowitz, McLaren, Macedo, Freire, and others to make perfectly good sense. But in the pause that I took, and I really did take one, I had to wonder why it was that these conservatives had done nothing whatsoever to change the funding of city school systems. Why they were not deeply concerned that schools in poorer areas of the United States suffer from overcrowding, a lack of materials, outdated textbooks, and empty library shelves. Why they felt a need to protect the literary canon from students who can barely read and write. I had to wonder why they had not railed against public schools in New York City (and other urban areas) that put 35 students in a classroom and expect teachers to teach five sections of these classes (175 students) per day. A warehouse by any other name is still a warehouse.

I had to wonder why it was that when the Bush administration generated *America 2000* that the first conservative response was to call for more testing: instead of asking how we might go about creating a highly literate American population, we would give tests to show—to show what (Courts and McInerney: 14–16)? It's an important question because the only thing that literacy tests could show is that the population is not anywhere near as literate as any of us would want it to be. So the tests would show failure. Whose failure? The failure of schools and teachers? Schools with 35 students per class and teachers who teach five of those classes per day? Schools in which students must pass through metal detectors before being allowed to enter because of the possibility (and in some areas likelihood) that some students will be carrying weapons? I have yet to see a response to *America 2000* from anyone in power that asks what we have to do to help teachers and students achieve any of the desirable objectives the document proposes.

But pauses being what they are, sometimes offering the opportunity for critical self-reflection, I also wondered if my own rhetoric and the rhetoric of some of those I read—not just conservatives—might not suffer from at least a small dose of self-righteousness. Through this kind of thinking it occurred to me that there is danger in believing so much in the potential good of critical pedagogy that I (and others?) just might fall into the trap of doing and becoming that which we argue against: i.e., just as Hirsch's notions about cultural literacy and his apparent belief that it can be forced on students seems oppressive, absurd, and counterproductive, so also is forced "liberation." The simple fact that a group of educators and theorists believe in the need for radical educational reform leading to critical/liberatory pedagogy and an active, *creative* cultural literacy is likely to have little currency with many of the students and parents of those students who populate the communities within which such radical change may need to occur. It was within this reflective moment, this moment of questioning my own place in the system and the ways in which it may construct me that I revisited Foucault's writings. He suggests that the intellectual's political agenda is as follows: "The essential problem for the intellectual is . . . ascertaining the possibility of constituting a new politics of truth. . . . It's not a matter of emancipating truth from every system of power (which would be a chimera, for truth is already power) but of detaching the power of truth from the forms of hegemony, social, economic and cultural, within which it operates at the present time" (*Power/Knowledge*: 133). And at least, in part, this is my intention in much that follows.

As this discussion moves toward an examination of some cultural "islands" on this continent, and in other chapters toward the experiences of some of the individuals in these other cultures (or Discourse communities), it is imperative that we maintain consciousness of the absolute impossibility to fully enter another culture. In a fascinating book examining the language and representation among North American Indians, David Murray expresses the difficult position the anthropologist or ethnographer is faced with: the "objective observer" turns the culture and the individuals within it into objects to be submitted to the "scientific" apparatus of the researcher; the participatory observer becomes subject along with the subjects under examination, losing distance and much hope of "objectivity." Consequently, those of us who read and write about cultural groups or Discourse communities must remember that we occupy a "gap" created by our attempt to be inside and outside of any given community at any given time (Murray, 1991). We might all do well to remember that generalizations about Discourse communities (Native Americans, African

Americans, Mexican Americans, Puerto Ricans, Appalachians, middle-class Anglos . . .) are only generalizations. As such they are filled with exceptions, particularly insofar as they are applied to individuals. And the same holds true for the generalizations made about liberal versus conservative educators in my earlier remarks. The danger of creating binary oppositions or of either villanizing or romanticizing through generalizations is a danger that haunts this book. As author, I would hope that readers react to all of the generalizations I make with a, "Yes, but . . . ." Having said this, let us look at some communities that, for one reason or another, have been separated from the dominant mainstream. For it is only as we look at genuine *difference* that we can begin to consider the complexity involved in teaching for critical consciousness (*conscientização*; Freire, 1973: 41; 1985: 185).

Consider, for example, Amish communities. I suspect that none of us would quickly assert that we have the right to liberate them educationally by forcing them into public schools that would violate the community's cultural and religious beliefs in addition to demanding that the Amish students acquire literacy characteristics that are not valued in the home community. But *if* we decided to "help" them join mainstream America, what might happen. Well, aside from the fact that they would experience culture shock and find many of their beliefs and traditions under attack, they would have more than a little trouble learning to adapt to literacy standards that violated those of their community. Amish children would be penalized or ignored in a public school because they focus on communication rather than on correctness, shun originality, and are unfamiliar with the 3rd person formal essay by virtue of living in a "first-person-plural society; thesis statements, topic sentences, and concepts like coherence, unity, and emphasis are similarly alien" (Fishman: 37). Of course, one might argue that, because the Amish *choose* to maintain their culture and community apart from, though within the larger culture, then they should be left to their own devices. Others might ask how much choosing is actually done if the children grow up in relative isolation as regards the larger culture. Regardless of how we look at it, however, if Amish children were forced into public

schools they would experience painful identity conflicts and
tension as they attempted to move between the world of public schooling and their home community.

But if the case of the Amish seems (literally) too isolated
and "different" from most other cases, it may simply be because we sometimes find it difficult to conceive of just how
different "others" might be, especially others that we forget
to remember or others whom we perceive from a distance
because we are not genuinely a part of their Discourse
community.

If we consider the Amish as existing on a kind of island
surrounded by the larger community, John Lofty's experience
teaching a group of junior high school students on an island
off the coast of Maine offers some loose points of comparison
(Lofty 1990). Lofty clearly enjoyed and respected his students,
but he was concerned about what appeared to be an unusual
resistance to writing. And noting that the students participated
happily in class discussions but "resisted writing," he examined the nature of that resistance (39), finding that the students attitudes toward school activities were strongly influenced
by community values, particularly on the ways in which this
fishing community viewed effective uses of time. For example,
prewriting made little sense to his students because the activity
seemed to be a waste of time to the students who, like their
parents, believed that when you start a job, you finish it: "Do it
until it's done" (40). Likewise, *revision* made little sense to these
students because they had been taught to do it right the first
time: "If it works, leave it alone" (41).

Lofty compares the students' approach to writing with the
process of quilt making or building a small boat, a process in
which the creator works with the materials immediately available, patching "together from what fits and works with little
concern for the intended purpose or the formal qualities of
the old" (42–43). Thus did his students weave together appro-
priated texts and tales they had heard in the community "with
scant regard for such conventions as a formally delineated
beginning, middle, and end" (43). Lofty notes that as the teachers would properly try to help the students develop broader
repertoires, the students viewed the teachers as violating the
students' sense of their ownership by asking that they do it the
teachers' way.

Deadlines and due dates were also problematic: from the students' point of view, school imposed artificial due dates; their community functioned more in terms of natural constraints. When the ice left the bay and the fishermen were able to get back to work, winter loans would be paid. When it was time to complete a writing assignment (i.e., "whenever I feel like it"), that is when it would get done and be handed in (44).

Lofty, of course, is not suggesting that the school simply give itself over to the community values, particularly because the island economy could not sustain the new generations of students and most of them would need to leave the island in order to get work. At this purely pragmatic level that often seems to drive the push for literacy, the teachers knew that the students needed to acquire more conventional literacy abilities, particularly in terms of their writing. To the extent that Lofty found a solution, it was based first in his recognition of the fact that his values and processes were different from those of his students. Once recognizing both the differences and the legitimacy of each set of values, he was able to involve his students in decision making and negotiations about how writing activities would proceed in the classroom. And as students become conscious of their own processes and approaches to the task, then and only then will alternative approaches be viewed as reasonable possibilities (47–48). Since I will be discussing classroom practices in a later chapter, I will not go into methodology here, but the point of this example is to compare it with the Amish situation and continue to question the role of the teacher in a "liberatory" teaching situation. One might argue that the Amish situation is quite different in that the Amish community successfully maintains its own members through the hard, communal work done by everyone within the community. Consequently, the young have no economic need to leave this "island" as did the young people Lofty describes. On the other hand, such a pragmatic, economic argument ignores the sometimes very harsh living conditions of many of the young people in some Amish communities.

Of course, if communities like those established by the Amish don't appear to be too unusual and isolated for serious consideration, we need only examine the circumstances of Native

Americans on this continent to further complicate matters. As
a colonized group Native Americans share similarities with
other colonized groups like many Mexican Americans, Puerto
Ricans or (once enslaved) groups like African Americans—but
there is a major difference. Native Americans are the only
group who have been legally granted their own property (reservations) and certain rights attendant to living and doing
business on that property (i.e., freedom from state sales taxes,
gasoline taxes, etc.). That these treaties have been regularly
violated over more than a century and that the Seneca Indians, for example, still find themselves in confrontation (sometimes violent) with people who have leased reservation lands
or with New York State authorities who want to tax them does
not change the fact that the Native American *island* is somewhat different from many of the other islands.

While it is undeniably true that many younger Native Americans do not speak the language of their forefathers, and some
know very little about the formalities associated with ritual
ceremonies, it is also true that much that characterized Native
Americans 150 years ago continues to influence actions,
thoughts, and attitudes of the people who live on some of the
larger reservations. The following discussion presents a few of
the differences that characterize some Native American communities—differences that fit poorly into the mainstream
American educational system (and other dominant institutions
as well). For example, Joseph Epes Brown explains how the
notion of interconnectedness and unity—a universal sense of
all embracing connection—pervades the belief systems of "all
Native American cultures" (Brown: 11). But schools are inherently fragmented and fragmenting, breaking the world of learning into 50 minutes of this subject followed by 50 minutes of
that subject and so on, with each 50 minutes and each subject
compartmentalized and separated from everything else in the
school. Likewise, many schools seldom make connections with
the lives that the students live outside of school.

In discussing Native American languages, Brown points out
that, "In Native languages the understanding is that the meaning *is* in the sound, it *is* in the word; the word is not a symbol
for a meaning which has been abstracted to, word and mean-

ing are together in one experience. Thus, to name . . . an animal [or anything] is actually to conjure up the powers latent in that animal" (13). Furthermore, because words are associated with breath, "the principle of life," the Native American "lends an added sacred dimension to the spoken word" (13). A person even mildly influenced to feel this way about language might be very hesitant to participate in various language activities that typify American schools. Imagine, for example, someone who believes in the sacredness of language practicing the writing of business letters. Likewise, remember that spoken language is emphasized here: as an historically oral culture, there is likely to be a very unwieldy fit with the world of artificial school language. (But isn't it exciting to consider the possibility of a school in which the utterances of students and teachers and custodians—a school in which everyone's language was considered to be sacred? Workbook drills would have to disappear because of their inherently trivializing and useless nature.)

Of course, as many of us already know, the nature of direct instruction and skills-drills that characterizes so many American schools offers little to experiential learners of any group. And to the extent that a community favored experiential learning, the school experience might be particularly problematic. In his essay, "Doing Your Own Thinking," Thomas Buckley points out that although Native American culture has been significantly influenced by European-American culture, it is most common for such influences to be "woven into the inclusive fabric of contemporary Indian life"; rather than eradicating the culture, the new ways are incorporated (36). For Native Americans, "*All* learning is experiential" (48). Direct instruction seldom occurs.

Having invited "yes, but . . ." responses earlier, I find myself having to add one right there. If all learning is experiential among Native Americans, then one might wonder why so much emphasis is put on oral storytelling in the culture. As is so often the case for me, the best answer I have been able to come up with involves paradoxes: for those of us who are accustomed to immersing ourselves in stories told or written by others, there is little confusion. Stories, spoken or written, are as experiential as the listener/reader is able to or chooses to make them. At the same time, *what* is learned through the "experience" of a story may be less clear.

In order to illustrate that last sentence, I have to begin by summarizing someone else's story—potentially a more hazardous undertaking than all the academic discussions of plagiarism generally suggest. Having spent more than 40 years studying the Navajo in southeastern Utah, living among them, marrying into Yellowman's family, learning the language, listening to and researching the Coyote stories, among a host of other things, Barre Toelken's observations strike like lightning in the desert. Even the disinterested observer is likely to notice.

Coyote is a fool: overindulging in sex and food, untrustworthy, dangerous to anyone who is around him. At first, Toelken thought the stories about Coyote were directed at children, intended to direct them toward good behavior. But he slowly came to realize that the stories were told only in winter, that they needed to be told or else the "children would grow up in a meaningless world," that they held great significance for the adults, and their degree of complexity went far beyond a child's capacity to understand. Toelken's interest in the stories and subsequent events cause him to re-think his entire involvement with the act of trying to "steal" other people's stories. He clearly points out that he was warned that his continuing desire to make the stories his own put him on a dangerous borderline, a line that once crossed moved him toward the Navajo conception of witchcraft, the symptoms of which, he explains are as follows: "extreme acquisitiveness, competition, aggressive behavior, selfishness, and the tendency to separate and dismantle those things which recognizably function as constellations of harmony. Personal recognition, analytical perspicacity, fame, tenure, money, and acclaim obviously do not appear on a list of healthy virtues for the Navajo" (33). Moreover, Toelken believes that he may have experienced some of the effects of practicing witchcraft insofar as his family and friends suffered through a series of devastating psychological and physical injuries while he was engaged in his "study" (33). Of course, this is nonsense. But then, everyone's belief system is nonsense (except, of course, my own).

Now, given the description of a witch in the above paragraph, we don't have to wonder too much about the way a person who believed in this description would react to an American public school (not to mention typical corporate or academic settings). But Toelken's experience taught him more than that. And this is the connection with the discussion of experiential learning immediately above. He points out that, although the people "believed the [Coyote] stories were true, they almost never saw the etiological ending of a story (e.g., that's how the bobcat got pointed ears) as being at all explanatory of anything. The meaning they believed in was that which was dramatized in the narrative itself" (29). In short, for all the insistence that the word is the thing itself, the stories operate at a clearly metaphorical level and must be interpreted for their true meaning, as did the warnings that Toelken was given when Yellowman cautioned him about his "scholarly" investigation (32).

Furthermore, I am faced with the deep irony that everything I am learning and writing about Native Americans (and many other groups I am discussing), with few exceptions, comes to me through print, not through the spoken word or immediate experience. Now that the stories are being written down, are they less true? Am I "stealing" them and endangering my family and friends? I do not think of myself as a witch, but then, neither did Toelken.

At times like this, it may seem odd to seek support from someone like Derrida, but so it goes.

The following quote from Derrida may, at first glance, seem to completely contradict the Native American notion that the *word* is one with that which it names. And, of course, it does directly contradict such a notion: Eurocentric positions often contradict beliefs of non-Eurocentric cultures. But most important for this discussion is to couple this contradiction with Derrida's notion of *supplement*. It seems reasonable to me to suggest that the Native American's desire for presence, the emphasis on an inherent relationship between language and reality represents an attempt to live in terms of the cultural belief system that emphasizes wholeness, unity, oneness, circularity; it is a reasonable attempt to stand solidly against a deconstructing universe:

> That substitution has always already begun; that imitation, principle
> of art, has always already interrupted natural plenitude; that having
> to be a *discourse*, it has always already broached presence in differ-
> ence; that in nature it is always that which supplies Nature's lack, a
> voice that is substituted for the voice of Nature. (Derrida: 215)

For me, then, there is an important difference between trying to steal someone's story and repeating it so that I can participate in the act of *supplement*. Indeed, where are the genuinely *new* stories? Consider what follows and think about this:
aren't stories almost always more interesting, more memorable
than the preacherly explanation of what they mean?

Simon J. Ortiz, for example, uses a story to explain the importance his Acoma Pueblo language plays in the essential nature of what it means to be Native American. Ortiz's sister told
him of a four-year-old boy who would not speak no matter how
much he was urged. Believing that there was something seriously wrong, the boy's sisters took him to their grandfather, "a
religious leader and healer" who "knew the art and science of
putting a person back into balance with the life of the
Aacquemeh hanoh." The grandfather tells the boy not to worry;
he will speak when it is time to speak. He assures him that
when he comes into language, he will use it to express love for
himself and his people, and this is how he "will come about as
a person." The grandfather then takes a brass key from his
pocket, inserts it into the boy's mouth and tells him that he
will now speak. According to Ortiz's sister, the boy started talking and never shut up since. Ortiz has a hunch that he was the
boy. But he tells the story to emphasize the "intimacy enhanced
by language," the closeness of the family and the role that the
oral tradition plays in that intimacy and closeness (Ortiz: 6–7):

> I'd heard stories all my life, ranging from the very traditional to the
> history of Acoma-Mericano relations to current gossip. Stories were
> told about people of the Aaquemeh community, our relatives, both
> living and long ago, and there were stories of mythic people and be-
> ings who were wondrous and heroic and even magical. Some stories
> were funny, some sad; all were interesting and vitally important to me
> because, though I could not explain it then, they tied me into the
> communal body of my people and heritage. I could never hear enough
> of the stories. (9)

Indeed, the stories are so important to Ortiz that they motivate his poetic attempts in *Going for the Rain* and *A Good Journey* to "instill that sense of continuity essential to the poetry and stories in the books, essential to Native American life" (9). Continuity, continuance, remembering, invoking the circle of being, for this Native American writer, represent "life itself" (9–10).

Of course, there are many important and illustrative stories about Native Americans, and given Toelken's warnings, it is important to remember that I can only re-tell: they are not mine, and I don't know if this next one is a genuinely new story, though it was new to me. A colleague and friend, Tom Malinowski, has a deep personal and scholarly interest in Native Americans, has been adopted into a tribe, given his own Indian name and song, and has participated in many ritual ceremonies. While he has many wonderful stories (but those are his for his book), his story of what occurred at a "pipe ceremony" is enlightening, particularly if one thinks about those students and their parents on that island off of Maine that Lofty writes about. In Lofty's story, the entire community had a sense of time that differed from that of mainlanders: for them time was directly related to seasons and when it was the *proper time* to do something. But back to the pipe ceremony.

Pipe ceremonies are serious stuff, highly ritualized moments affirming the interconnectedness of all who sit in the circle and share the smoke. (See Arthur Amiotte, "The Road to the Center" in Dooling and Jordan-Smith, 246-254 for a powerful description of the pipe ceremony as celebrated in the ceremony known as the Sun Dance.) As is typical of many rituals, the pipe ceremony is conducted slowly and meticulously, each step and each element (the pipe itself, the tobacco, the song . . .) receiving full attention and respect. It can also be a relatively long ceremony. In this particular story, after about ten or so minutes into the ceremony, a newcomer joined the circle, and because each person must experience the ceremony in full, everything had to begin again. Once again, the ceremony began, only to be reinterrupted by another latecomer—though "latecomer" is probably the wrong word here. Again, the ritual was begun. Several newcomers later, my friend was beginning to think that he may have become a part of an unending pipe-smoking ceremony, as the ceremony was begun again for each newcomer.

Although there are a variety of genuinely interesting points involved in the story, I will highlight only a few (it's not my story, and this is, after all, an academic book, so I have to be preacherly). The newcomers were not really *late* because, in this culture, you get to where you are supposed to be when you get there. Things get done when it is time to get them done. And there is always time to celebrate unity and to avoid fragmentation. That such a sense of time makes for a frustrating fit when these same people are "late" or absent for work or school can come as little surprise: "Of course I was not here; I had to gut and dress the deer we shot!"

That such attitudes as these that characterize some Native Americans seem to fly directly in the face of what is valued in a technocratic, capitalistic, and progressive society is pretty obvious. But if you believe that much that characterizes technocracies, capitalism, and progress is closely related to the Navajo notion of witchcraft, then . . . ?

But on to another "island," one that offers additional points for comparison at the same time it adds more layers of complexity to the issue. James Moffett examines the censoring of textbooks that took place in Kanawha County, West Virginia, in 1974, when one segment of the school community found itself deeply offended by the textbooks, objectives, and practices of the local public schools (Moffett, 1990). Using every means at their disposal, including violence, these people attempted to censor both the textbooks and teaching approaches used in the schools. The event sparked tremendous anger and hostility as the community and religious values of the "fundamentalist ministers from the hills and hollows of the upper valley" and their followers pulled their students out of school, threatened others who did not do the same, protested and disobeyed court injunctions, and participated in disruptive acts even to the extent of resorting to the use of guns and the firebombing of schools (113–114). As is admirably typical of Moffett, he conducts his examination with genuine respect for those who were so angered as he tries to understand the reasons these people were so terribly upset with the schools and their textbooks and programs, of which his K–12 "Interaction" program was a part.

Moffett finds that the parents were afraid that they would lose their children who were being "mentally kidnapped by voices from other milieus and ideologies" (114). These fundamentalist parents found the topics and questions English teachers were introducing to their children to be invasive, confusing, and essentially raising issues that the parents considered "already settled" in terms of their own "religious beliefs and values" (114). Attempts to engage students in readings, writings, and discussions about pluralism, multiculturalism, personal writing, and so on simply represented "an effort to indoctrinate their children in the atheistic freethinking of the Eastern-seaboard liberal establishment that scoffs at them and runs the country according to a religion of secular humanism" (114–115).

By examining this particularly charged moment, and by bothering to care about the people that liberals and conservatives alike so often dismiss as ignorant hillbillies, Moffett provides a ground on which to formulate some terribly important questions. Unlike the students on the island off the coast of Maine that Lofty (1990) writes about, the West Virginia uproar grows out of the overt, expressed religious beliefs and values of a major segment of the community. It is also terribly important to note that many people in the community did not share the values and beliefs of the fundamentalists: i.e., this was not like an Amish community in which everyone shared a set of established beliefs and values (Apple: 197). The schools and teachers, then, were firmly caught in the middle of a kind of culture war. And it is exactly this kind of situation that allows us to think directly about the complexities that we introduce when we ask students to engage in an ideological examination of their own culture and the surrounding dominant culture. The acts of inquiry and examination, in and of themselves, may violate the traditions and beliefs of the people who live in some of the communities we most want to affect.

I want to use these examples offered by Toelken, Moffett, Lofty, Villanueva and others to problematize some of the positions that are often associated with liberatory education: I do so, *not* as an attempt to undercut critical pedagogies, but as an attempt to highlight what I believe are powerful complexities that are implicit in any liberatory movement, especially in an educational system in which school attendance is required by law. In an important book, *Culture and Power in the Classroom*, Antonia Darder, accurately writes that critical pedagogy intends to help "students develop the critical capacities to reflect, critique, and act to transform the conditions under which they live" (xvii). After critiquing the problems with conservative educational discourse, she also presents a critique of a "liberal educational discourse" as something of a mirror image of the conservative program: "While the conservative perspective disempowers students through its insistence on an objective and neutral view of knowledge, the liberal discourse commits a similar offense in reverse. With its heavy emphasis on individual subjectivity, it fails to move beyond a relativistic notion of knowledge and hence disregards the ideological structural constraints of the dominant culture that informs school practices which function to the detriment of many students of color. . . . Consequently, in spite of its humanistic posture, the traditional liberal discourse also degenerates into an ahistorical, undialectical, and apolitical view that functions ultimately to curtail the forms of critical thinking and productive education for bicultural students" (10–11).

Of course some "liberal" teachers may fulfill Darder's characterization, and to the extent they do so, they are failing their students. And it would be relatively easy to misrepresent Darder by presenting the above quotes out of context: the fact is that she clearly understands the problems that teachers deal with on a daily basis in the schools and she presents some important ideas for changes that might and I think should take place in classrooms. But my point here is to examine the hidden conflict and genuine ironies that are inherent in "liberal" and/ or liberatory approaches to education. My reason for doing so is this: without a direct examination of paradoxes and ironies, without an honest examination of the critical theories that underlie liberatory/critical pedagogies as they interface with real communities and real students and teachers, the movement is likely to fail and/or stay cloistered in the world of academic publication.

Some Complexities

First consider this, in much that is written by those who associate themselves with critical or liberatory pedagogy, schools are often presented as representative of the dominant societal discourse of white (male) upper-middle class America; they are presented as institutions that essentially short circuit real learning in favor of the memorization-recitation of fragmented and therefore useless bits of discrete knowledge. And they are generally presented as institutions whose main objective is to maintain the status quo, including the status of illiterate or semiliterate minorities. Whether schools are consciously constructed in this manner or not, I find it hard to disagree with the factual bases for such negative descriptions.

Second, critical pedagogy is normally viewed as an attempt to radically reform schools as characterized in the above paragraph, engaging students in the highly political act of examining their own and others' cultures, the influence of the dominant culture as it (mis)shapes their existence, and the need for them to take constructive action as agents of cultural, social, and economic change. It is a pedagogy of conflict in which the students and teachers actively confront a dominant, dominating society and its oppressive attitudes toward the poor, minorities, gays, and just about anyone or anything that represents "difference." And it is a movement with which I associate myself and my teaching.

But the West Virginia schools that Moffett describes, though hardly bastions of radical, critical theory and practice, were trying to engage the real lives of their students and involve the students in a critical examination and reflection of their own values and the values of the larger dominant culture. In point of fact, these schools, instead of fulfilling the traditional conservative educational agenda of turning out good little Americans who will stay in their assigned societal seats and unquestioningly serve the market place (if they are allowed in)—these schools were inviting students to engage in more complex literacy activities so that they might question and make decisions about cultural givens. But the invitation conflicted directly with the values and religious beliefs of the fundamentalist Christians creating a situation in which the teachers' attempts to help students become aware of their own culture and the dominating elements of the larger culture that controls them became perceived as an *attack* on the subculture. In short, the schools were attempting to liberate people who saw such liberation as a central danger to everything they are as a community.

Of course, neither Moffett nor I suggest that we simply throw up our hands in defeat and take on a naive, relativistic position by suggesting that we must simply leave these students alone and avoid trying to help them learn to be constructive, critical thinkers and active agents in their own lives and the lives of those around them, deciding about beliefs and values instead of simply receiving them as (God) given. To do so would come dangerously close to the "happy slave" argument: "They enjoy the way they live so leave them alone!" But I would certainly suggest that we cannot afford to be trapped in our own righteousness by deciding that we should (can) turn the students into good little cultural workers dedicated to overthrowing the oppressive capitalists who are exploiting the poor Appalachians of West Virginia. And it is not that I do not *hope* that they might radically change the system of oppression that entraps them; I simply believe that it is not my decision, or anyone else's, to make *for* them.

By the same token, I agree with Darder who suggests that we must also avoid the trap of simply encouraging everyone to muddle around in solipsistic personal narratives and self-reflection pretending that I'm Okay and You're Okay and everything is just dandy. As Ortiz points out, alcoholism and violence are common on Native American reservations, powerful symptoms of the erosion of cultural identity caused by the treatment of these peoples by the powerful system that sent them to live on those reservations. Danger, death, and drugs surround the people who live in the ghettoes Villanueva mentions. Many Appalachians are trapped in urban ghettoes characterized by poverty and highly inadequate health care. On the other hand, none of us can ignore one of the central West Virginia lessons: the poor and the minorities of America are not waiting breathlessly for us to liberate them through education. Indeed the false promise of the marketplace works so well that many people resist liberation because they so fervently believe and hope that they can gain the mobility to enter the mainstream of the dominant society and share the wealth. And in many ways, this is exactly the kind of paradox that causes Lisa Delpit to take the position she does when she complains about white educators who appear unwilling to listen to black educators describe the needs of their black students (Delpit: 1986, 1988, 1992). In short, the conflicts and oppositions involved in critical education are more than a little complex and involve considerably more than a conflict between the oppressed minorities and an oppressive socioeconomic system. And this is particularly true when we move from theoretical positions to concrete realities involving actual practices in the schools with real human beings.

I believe that Moffett's own words best suggest the kinds of care that we all need to take as we work in the fields of cultural and socioeconomic change so that they can be growing fields instead of the killing fields that have characterized so many cultural intrusions from Vietnam to Bosnia to Iraq to Cambodia to Palestine to . . . . Moffett writes: "Transmit the culture, yes, but subordinate that to transcending the culture. . . . The world is warring right and left because the various cultures strive so intently to perpetuate themselves that they end by imposing themselves on each other. These lethal efforts to make others like oneself burlesque the expanded identity that would make possible real global unity. The secret of war is that nations need enemies to maintain definition, because differences define" (1990: 119). As educators, we need to encourage and sustain difference, when possible, without encouraging or creating enemies.

At the same time, having issued these cautions, let us also be fully aware that the conservative agenda of the Hirschs, Bennetts, Cheneys, Ravitches, and Buchanans of this world *requires the conceptualizing of DIFFERENCE AS ENEMY*, the identification and elimination of difference, and the subordination of anyone who chooses to be outside their camps. Interestingly enough, one of the ways of implementing such an agenda is the call for assessment of schools and students, a movement that might be constructive were it managed by teachers and students working together, but most often is destructive because it is managed by the corporate testing structure best represented by the profit making conglomerates known as Princeton Testing and American College Testing (Courts and McInerney, 1993).

Assessment and Standards: Say what?

Now I ask you, who could be against standards? And if you have standards, which you must if you are a good American, then you must be in favor of assessing whether or not people are performing up to the standards. And where better than to focus issues of assessment and standards than in the schools?

In actuality, of course, the setting of educational standards and the assessing of them are overtly political areas in which ironies abound.

As one who has long been involved in educational assessment of student learning, primarily forced into such involvement in order to create defensive positions against all those conservative attacks on teachers and students, I remain somewhat amazed that the emphasis on assessment is often accompanied by an utter disregard for supplying the support necessary to make changes in education. For example, an experience I still find more than a little ironic occurred when my colleagues and I presented papers on qualitative assessment of students' learning at a conference sponsored by the State University of New York at Albany in October 1993 (Amiran and Courts, 1994). At the final session of the conference, after the sponsoring bureaucrats finished their speech making, those of us who had participated were allowed to ask some questions of those who run the State University of New York system. I pointed out that some of the institutions represented at the Conference had been conducting assessment projects for several years, and our results suggested pretty clearly that in the area of language and literacy, we needed to have smaller classes so professors could work more with students' reading and writing processes. I asked when we might stop having conferences about how to do assessment and start getting some support from the state to implement what successful assessment projects clearly indicated we needed to do.

I was answered by a vice chancellor of SUNY who said that I couldn't expect a pay raise for having been involved in assessment. I still don't know what he thought I said, but that ended the "discussion." And mind you, there are witnesses to this event. Not once, never in the entire Conference did anyone address the issue of *providing support to make the changes that must be made* if we are to improve education at any level.

But let me generalize from this experience very directly: Presumably we assess in order to find out how well we and our students are doing. When we identify problem areas and conceive possible solutions, we implement those solutions. "Presumably" is a very important word here. In fact, what appears to be happening, nationwide, is that assessment, especially qualitative assessment that actually gives us some real information, seems to occur for nothing more than the sake of doing assessment. In my university system, assessment concretely revealed the need for smaller classes, more interactive and collaborative learning, an emphasis on writing across disciplines, and a need for multicultural studies across disciplines. The response has been to raise class size, eliminate faculty, make it considerably more difficult for minorities to be able to afford to go to college, and so on. At least *ironic*, wouldn't you say? Furthermore, it takes little administrative insight to figure out what happens to women's studies or multicultural studies programs in the face of downsizing that threatens the traditional core of higher education. Perhaps *ironic* is not quite the right word?

At present, for example, the entire State University of New York system is experiencing "downsizing" (interesting word, that) in order to "improve" our services. In actuality, this means the closing of campuses, loss of faculty, larger class sizes, raises in tuition, and less financial support throughout the state for poorer families who might hope to send their children to college. Lest I appear to be creating a fiction, here, I offer the following statements written by Candace de Russy (a newly appointed trustee) in a memorandum sent to her fellow Trustees of the State University of New York. Candace de Russy writes: "SUNY has contributed to the decline of public education," apparently as a result of an "unbridled interpretation of 'access'" (2). I think she is referring to minority students when she speaks of *unbridled access*, but instead of inferring what de Russy means by these statements, it is only fair to use her own words as follows:

1. De Russy suggests that SUNY "Eliminate any English-as-a-Second-Language courses" (3).
2. Perhaps understanding such a suggestion might appear racist at worst and isolationist at best, de Russy quotes the "late and distinguished CUNY professor, Barry Gross: who wrote in a New York Times Op-Ed piece (April 22, 1995) as follows: 'Why should students who speak minimal English be admitted to higher education?'" (3).
3. De Russy goes on to call for more "faculty productivity," "raising tuition [again]," "expanding privatization [i.e., cutting tax support]," in addition to the need to "Review race- and sex-based preferences [in admissions procedures]" (4–6).

Something is indeed happening here, and I believe even Bob Dylan's fictional Mr. Jones would find a weatherman unnecessary. These kinds of statements from a trustee of one of the finest state university systems in the Unites States suggest that we had better put our trust elsewhere if we have any hope of providing high quality education for those who populate minority groups and lower income brackets. Cost cutting is one thing, but when it is surrounded with statements about "academic standards," "unbridled access," and an attack on affirmative action policies and bilingualism, even the dim of wit can identify a hidden agenda that isn't very well hidden.

And as this memorandum clearly emphasizes, we all need to be deeply concerned with educational standards—one of the favorite issues of those conservatives I mentioned above. Anyone familiar with the educational landscape knows that "assessment" and "standards" have been in the limelight for many years now (Hutchings and Marchese, 1990; Courts and McInerney, 1993; Daniels, 1994). Indeed, with so many people interested in testing and assessing educational standards, one would expect that the issue would have been settled, but the fact is that discussions of standards in education almost always reflect major compromises among warring factions, oftentimes with considerable influence coming from factions whose interest in helping our children is at least suspect. For example, as Harvey Daniels points out: "The College Board and 'research' departments of ETS have long been tweedy Trojan Horses, conducting ostensibly altruistic investigations which somehow usually result in new products which make money for ETS and tighten the choke hold that standardized tests have on the throat of school reform in this country" (Daniels, 1994: 47).

Indeed, the entire issue of testing and "standards setting" is a fascinating and revealing one to explore. Consider, for example, the discussions surrounding the standards projects launched by two education groups and funded by the government: one group, the National Center for History in the Schools (NCHS) was revising curriculum guidelines for history teachers; the other group involved a collaborative effort between The National Council of Teachers of English (NCTE), the largest professional organization of English teachers from elementary school through graduate school, and The International Reading Association (IRA), with a large membership of elementary, high school, and college teachers. To the best of my knowledge, neither group is generally considered to be particularly subversive, especially given the fact that each group and their respective memberships are devoted to improving the language and literacy abilities of the nation's children and adults. (But then again, genuine literacy and a constructive understanding of our county's history may represent subversiveness to those bent on constructing star-spangled fictions.)

The National Endowment for the Humanities had funded the history standards project, directing the National Center for History in the Schools (NCHS) to create curriculum standards for the teaching of history in American schools. Unfortunately, conservatives didn't like the outcome and their criticisms are represented by remarks made by Lynn Cheney, former chair of the NEH and a person partly responsible for the initial funding: "In a *Wall Street Journal* commentary, Cheney said the standards for the study of U.S. history present a 'warped and distorted version of the American past in which it becomes a story of oppression and failure.' After NCHS released its standards for the study of world history, Cheney said they reflected 'the same kind of bias against the West that you had in the history of the U.S.'" In a related attack, Cheney fires at "Cal Poly English professor Donald Lazere" as follows: "This faculty member is determined to convert his students to his point of view. He has no intention of introducing them to other perspectives. He wants students to embrace his conviction that the United States is a closed and class-ridden society, and he intends to bring them to this realization while they are in his class" (*Council Chronicle*, June 1995: 12). Making this statement in both her final report as NEH chair, "Telling the Truth: A Report on the State of the Humanities in Higher Education" and in a "Republican Issues Conference talk broadcast on C-SPAN," Cheney apparently chose to disregard what Lazere wrote in the article of his she attacks. Lazere writes: "Conservatives are correct in insisting that it is illegitimate for teachers to advocate a revolutionary or any other ideological position in a one-sided way and to force that position on students—and despite the tendentious exaggerations of conservative critics about the tyranny of left political correctness, this sometimes does occur" (*Council Chronicle*, June 1995: 12).

Little wonder, then, that in January, "the U.S. Senate passed a nonbinding resolution by a vote of 99–1 that national history education standards shouldn't be based on those developed by NCHS" (*Council Chronicle*, April 1995: 1). From a conservative perspective, NCHS came up with the wrong standards; some folks just never get it right.

Likewise, work of The National Council of Teachers of English and The International Reading Association seems to have displeased the conservative power structure. Apparently, those in power at the Department of Education expected a set of standards that would return language and literacy studies in the schools to the drills and skills models of the past (and often the present). They also apparently had hoped that the canon of Western literature would be reinstated, thus stemming the "dangerous" groundswell of interest in multiculturalism and literatures produced by authors (male *and* female), who represent *and write about* ethnic, national, religious, sexual, economic, sociological, and political diversity—authors who represent groups who for much too long have had little or no representation in the texts students read in our schools and colleges. In addition, the governmental trend setters apparently expected this group of teachers and scholars in the areas of language and literacy to simply forget about or ignore the enormously important pedagogical changes that have grown out of 40 years of research in linguistics, psycho- and sociolinguistics, cognitive psychology, discourse theory, critical theory, and educational theory. These powerful conservatives also, apparently, expected the NCTE/IRA panel members to forget their own years of experience as teachers of language and literacy. To put it simply, the Department of Education did not like what the NCTE/IRA folks were producing, so they eliminated support and funding.

One can only guess that some government agencies and conservative educational spokespersons like Cheney believe that "standards" should be created and implemented without the thinking and experience of teachers and scholars in the field. Likewise, one inference seems unavoidable: if you are going to be involved in a standards project funded by a government agency, ask them exactly what it is you are supposed to write so you can get it right the first time! Indeed, the pedagogical and political split over the establishing of standards is clearly illustrated in the response of conservatives to the publication of *The Standards for the English Language Arts*, the result of the joint project of the National Council of Teachers of English and the International Reading Association. Deeply upset that this new standards statement did not identify "a common body of knowledge that binds us all together," and that it did not emphasize lists of discrete, fragmented skills that must be evidenced at specific grade levels, conservatives voiced their opposition (McLeary: 1). It is relatively clear that much of the hostility directed at this new statement of standards grows out of its respectful inclusion of cultural and linguistic diversity as well as its demonstration of a clear understanding of the nature of literacy and language development, and the flexibility necessary when discussing standards in such complex areas of learning. But one also wonders if part of the hostility is not raised by the fact that the NCTE/IRA statement notes the need for society and politicians to do something concrete about establishing equitable learning environments for our young people. As the writers of the report point out, "standards, by themselves, cannot erase the impact of poverty, ethnic and cultural discrimination, family illiteracy, and social and political disenfranchisement" ("Standards": 9). One cannot help but wonder if Shanker, Finn, Ravitch, Dole, and a host of others are not longing for a reinstatement of the kinds of skill and competency based standards, tied to grade levels and tested by standardized multiple choice tests that characterized the 1950s, 1960s and 1970s (for the conservative perspective, see the *American Educator* Spring 1996 issue, entirely devoted to "the Standards Movement").

As Harvey Daniels, points out, none of this is terribly surprising. Why would those of us interested in educational change expect honest, ethical, open-minded support from governmental agencies whose job it is to serve and maintain the status quo. We might, for example, simply ask ourselves this: What do you really think the leadership in the Department of Education (or just about any major arm of the federal and most state governmental agencies) actually thinks about classroom teachers? The answer comes easily and clearly if we skip political rhetoric and simply look at the funding patterns for education throughout the nation at all levels over the past several decades. In what major cities or state systems of higher education have class sizes gone down? In what areas has support for minorities and poor people gone up? Those who want carefully articulated standards established for all learners seem to care little about establishing equitable funding for the schools many of these learners and teachers occupy.

For those of us who care deeply about students and education and the future, the ironies and contradictions created by the political/educational leadership can no longer be tolerated. If Diane Ravitch asks, "'What does class analysis have to do with education when we live in a classless society?'" we must loudly point out that only in a carefully constructed "classed" society could people like her make decisions that powerfully affect the lives of people who will never be allowed to enter her class. And when William Bennett says that, "Race, class, and gender studies are inappropriate in our schools," we must recognize that he sees them to be inappropriate because his own power base depends on the avoidance of such studies (Kincheloe, et al., in Macedo 1994: xiv) .

On the other hand, it is all too easy to get caught up in arguing with and about people like Bennett, Hirsch, Ravitch, etc. In many ways, to focus on them as part of a binary opposition, them on one side and us on the other, is to stay firmly entrenched in the hegemonic forces they represent. We need, I believe, to remember Foucault's description of "domination":

"in speaking of domination I do not have in mind that solid and global kind of domination that one person exercises over others, or one group over another, but the manifold forms of domination that can be exercised within society. Not the domination of the King in his central position, therefore, but that of his subjects in their mutual relations: not the uniform edifice of sovereignty, but the multiple forms of subjugation that have a place and function within the social organism" (1980: 96). And of those "multiple forms of subjugation," I would argue that language and discourse systems are among the most important to examine.

We must take up the constructive challenges issued by Freire, Giroux, Aronowitz, Macedo, McLaren, Darder, Smitherman, and many other fine writers associated with liberatory pedagogy and move those challenges into discussions of the kind of changes that must begin to characterize our classrooms. From my own perspective as someone who is primarily interested in language and literacy, accepting such a challenge demands, first and foremost, an understanding of the nature of language. All of us need to examine the important differences in the ways that people use language in their attempt to become active participants in their own lives and the lives of those around them. And at the same time, remembering Foucault's "multiple forms of subjugation," we must examine the ways in which *language uses us*. Consequently, in the following chapter, we will look at issues related to standard and non-standard English, dialects, and Discourse systems.

Several reminders and cautions are, however, necessary before I proceed.

Noam Chomsky has said that schools are "institutions for indoctrination, for imposing obedience, for blocking the possibility of independent thought, and they play an institutional role in a system of control and coercion. Real schools ought to provide people with techniques of self-defense, but that would mean teaching the truth about the world and about society, and schools couldn't survive very long if they did that" (Chomsky: 671). Of course, teaching "the truth" about anything is difficult and faces those of us who teach with some complex questions: Whose truth? How do we avoid simply becoming another system of indoctrination? Didn't Mao's Red

Guard do exactly the same thing with a vengeance? How do we avoid allowing the revolution to become more repressive than that which was overthrown? These are all important questions and they must be faced, but at the same time it is worth noting that the "oppressors" are doing a wonderful job of resisting change of any kind, let alone revolutionary change. On the other hand, perhaps we might come considerably closer to helping students discover truths if we avoided teaching lies, if we actively engaged our students, at all levels, in a straightforward examination of the world in which we live.

I became more than a little worried about *truth* as I moved forward in the researching and writing of this book. What follows in the book is an examination of how cultures shape the Discourse systems of those within them, how different people and their different Discourse systems are treated in schools, and finally, some suggestions about how they might be better and more constructively treated in schools. Speaking/writing the *truth* about language is always a sticky proposition, and I don't pretend to know the truth about the language and Discourse of any given culture. Consequently, at no point do I intend the mention of characteristics of a group or a culture, linguistic or otherwise, to imply that all individuals within the group possess all or any of a given set of characteristics. Human beings are wonderfully various, and while they are, to a great extent, constructed by their environment, they are also inherently creative and fully capable of constructing themselves (Courts, 1991). My point here and throughout the book is to present windows that allow readers to consider the broad varieties of human dialects and Discourse systems that are, by virtue of being different from the dominant mainstream, repressed in the schools.

Chapter 2

Dialects and Discourses: Dig?

"Why should the *Palatine Boors* be suffered to swarm into our Settlements and, by herding together, establish their Language and Manners, to the Exclusion of ours? Why should *Pennsylvania*, founded by the *English*, become a Colony of *Aliens*, who will shortly be so numerous as to Germanize us instead of our Anglifying them?" (Benjamin Franklin quoted in G. Weaver: 57)

Now, it ain nothin wrong with being "uplifted," but the miseducation comes in when we attempt to answer the questions: uplifted *from* what? *to* what? In the language area, teaching strategies which seek only to put white middle-class English into the mouths of black speakers ain did nothin to inculcate the black perspective necessary to address the crises in the black community. (Smitherman, 1977: 209)

It is simplistic and to our detriment as educators of bicultural students to accept the notion that any one particular form of language (i.e., "standard" English), in and of itself, constitutes a totalizing dominant or subordinate force, as it is unrealistic to believe that simply utilizing a student's primary language (e.g., Spanish, Ebonics, etc.) guarantees that a student's emancipatory interests are being addressed. (Darder, 1991: 102)

The following explores a variety of complex, related issues having to do with language and discourse systems. While much of the information on American English dialects is not at all new to linguists, it is necessary to present it as background for those readers who may know little about socio- and applied linguistics. In part, the discussion will focus on the kinds of bias and discrimination that come into play when authorities in dominant, mainstream institutions make judgments about the intelligence and quality of students' speaking and writing (thinking) abilities based on misinformation, prejudice, and often ignorance with regard to important aspects of socio- and applied linguistics. Initially, the discussion focuses on the nature of standard and non-standard dialects in the United States and the kinds of biases and confusions that are played out on the field of language. More specifically, I intend to examine the roles that schools and teachers play as they (mis)shape the discourse structures (and lives) of the minority and foreign students who populate classrooms from kindergarten through graduate school.

Aside from the fact that the issues I intend to discuss are emotionally and culturally "loaded," rife with undercurrents of racism, sexism, and classism (some of which are not very deeply submerged), the topic presents more than a few difficulties. One of the immediate difficulties presented by such an exploration is this: many of the terms necessary for the discussion are sometimes confused and confusing, especially because they are used in various ways by different people. For example, consider the following terms: "dialect," "standard English," "non-standard English," "Discourse systems," and "academic" or "essayist" literacy.

Dialects: "Why white folks always talking that jive shit?"

Dialects are associated with "speech communities," including relatively localized communities (neighborhood, school, office, profession) and larger communities like regions of the country (southeastern, Midwest) or areas in a city or state (southern Ohio, the southside of Chicago). Likewise, as Roger Shuy points out, "social layers [of dialects] exist *within* regional dialect areas. That is, well-educated, partly-educated, and uneducated people may all live within the boundaries of a well-defined dialect area," but they are likely to evidence dialect variations in matters of vocabulary, syntax, and pronunciation (Shuy: 3). Thus we can speak of *regional dialects*, dialects associated with geographic areas, and *social* dialects associated with characteristics of people within regions: "A dialect, then, is a variety of a language. It differs from other varieties in certain features of pronunciation, vocabulary, and grammar ('grammar' [meaning] . . . both word construction *and* syntax). It may reveal something about the social or regional background of its speakers, and it will be generally understood by speakers of other dialects of the same language" (Shuy: 4).

Dialect refers to both the deep structure (underlying rules for generating the language) and surface structures (the words and phrases as they are actually produced) of a group's *oral* language: that is, dialects vary in lexicon, phonology, and syntax (Wolfram: 45). I stress oral language, here, because, while it would not be unusual to find some features of a person's dialect showing up in his/her writing, it would be somewhat unusual (nearly impossible) for all the features of an oral dialect to evidence themselves in a person's writing, particularly phonological features, given the complexities of sound-symbol relationships in the English language. I will, however, discuss some important relationships between dialects and how a dialect may affect a student's linguistic performance later in this chapter.

Perhaps one of the most common misconceptions about dialects is the belief that one given dialect is inherently better than another. What follows, almost automatically, from such a misconception is a set of assumptions about the personal qualities, character, educational levels, economic status, etc. about people who speak a given dialect. In short, judgment of people in terms of their dialects is one of the many ways in which racial, class, sexual, and personal biases evidence themselves in our society. A second major misconception about dialects, deriving at least in part from the first one is that there is a standard (good) dialect that people who talk "correctly" speak, and then there are all those non-standard dialects spoken by people who "do not know any better." And this misconception is at least partly derived from the fact that most people do not realize that dialects have describable grammars (just like standard English), and that speakers of any given dialect have the same ability to generate and communicate ideas as any other speakers. As Conklin and Lourie point out, standard English is difficult to define specifically because it is essentially "the language of the powerful," and is often "wrongly sanctified as logically, expressively, and aesthetically superior" to other variants (97). They also explain that part of the reason it is difficult to define standard English "with any degree of precision" resides in the inherent nature of language change and regional variation (98). Finally, they suggest that, while written language appears to allow for fewer "acceptable" variations, "for both written and spoken standard American English, there is a firm national conviction that such a variety exists but a much shakier consensus on exactly what its characteristics are" (99).

Of course, there are also plenty of people who hold tightly to their language biases even when they know that dialects like the one often called "Black Vernacular" have definable grammars and are as capable of syntactic and semantic complexity as any other dialect. Indeed, the general definition of *non-standard* dialects derives from language bias: "Socially stigmatized features, then, are those linguistic items that negatively affect the listener's judgment of the speaker's social status. In Labov's scheme, these are the features classified as social markers or social stereotypes, not those classified as social indicators. Nonstandard speech, then, is speech containing socially stigmatized linguistic features" (Blanton: 79; see also Labov, 1964: 102).

But the simple fact is that no dialect is inherently better than another (though it is not unusual for individuals to feel that their own dialect is "best," and in a very real sense, the dialect that works best for you in a given language community may be "best"). All people have a dialect and some are able to employ features of different dialects when it serves certain social purposes. One important point surrounding dialects is this: no individual evidences all the characteristics of a given dialect. That is, individuals who speak Black Vernacular do not all speak the same way. Some evidence more marked phonological features than others. A non-standard dialect speaker from Harlem will display differences in vocabulary, phonology, and syntax when compared with a non-standard speaker from rural Alabama. Someone who grew up speaking Black Vernacular but who has been educated in largely white schools and colleges may still evidence a few non-standard markers in speech, but not nearly as many as an individual who stays within the original non-standard language community. And it is not unusual for some speakers to consciously try to maintain features of their original dialect even though they live and work in a different dialect community: southerners who are proud of their southern heritage may try to maintain certain features of their original dialect even though they have moved north;

immigrants from Mexico or Quebec (etc.) may maintain certain dialect features as part of a nationalistic or ethnic statement. By and large, however, most of us change our dialects to adapt to and become part of new discourse communities (dialect convergence) just as we often participate in the traditions and customs of the new community.

But language convergence does not always occur, and sometimes we find evidence of language *divergence*, unless, of course, we are segregated within a community or stopped from participating fully within the new community. As Dennis Preston points out, language convergence is less likely and divergence more likely when the minority group wishes to establish an identity separate from that of the majority, a fact that may explain "claims that Black and White vernaculars in urban northern American cities are diverging" (88).

As with non-standard dialects, no individual speaks "standard English," but speakers of standard English normally do not evidence many of the dialect features that characterize non-standard dialects, and they particularly attempt to avoid stigmatizing dialectal characteristics—characteristics that they feel indicate little education or an ethnic background against which the mainstream is biased. *Standard English* is the language of the people who represent the dominant power structure. Some people associate standard English with "Network English": "Newscasters are taught to use 'network English,' which has nearly uniform features of grammar and similar pronunciation features from coast to coast. The existence of network English causes most Americans to feel there is a national norm for English usage. Yet many personally identify more closely with the leaders of their own community than with national leaders and may therefore strive to imitate the local standard" [which for people living in a linguistic ghetto would be the non-standard dialect prominent in the community] (Conklin and Lourie: 98, 101). In point of fact, standard English includes different dialects, but it is most commonly associated with the language spoken by educated, upper-middle class whites in our society. Non-linguists, however, regularly stereotype others in terms of their speech, with "Network English" generally being regarded as best (Preston: 50). One vocal educator, Lisa Delpit, prefers to avoid the term "Standard English" altogether:

> What I talk about is edited English, which essentially is the English you see in books—English that has been taken through an editing process. Some people's home language is more closely related to edited English than other people's, but nobody exactly speaks edited English.

It's important to make the distinction because edited English is the language of power. If you don't have access to edited English, you don't have access to the power institutions in this country. (Delpit, 1992: 12)

But the color of one's skin, one's race, one's ethnicity, etc. have nothing inherent to do with whether or not one speaks standard or variant forms of English. Indeed, both non-standard dialects and standard English are primarily affected by the home environment and area in which a speaker is raised and the dialect that is dominant in that area. Just as French children in France grow up speaking a French that differs from the French spoken in Quebec, so also do children in Georgia speak a different dialect from those raised in Massachusetts or Texas. And quite commonly, children raised in affluent, literate households speak differently from those raised in homes characterized by poverty and illiteracy. But speakers of standard English *generally* evidence the inflected endings of English (markers for past participles, plurals, possessives, verb tenses, etc.), and by and large frown on those who say something like, "Marvin, he take John book and tear it all up the other day. And John, he mad." The word *generally* in the previous sentence, however, is very important because most speakers eliminate many word endings and change words into non-standard constructions in casual speech: "have to" becomes "hafta," "used to" becomes "usta," "desk" becomes "des," and so on.

Non-standard English includes all variants of the language that differ markedly from the language of the educated, upper-middle class, and these variations are often mistakenly assumed to evidence low intelligence, laziness, and illiteracy, among other things. Or to put it differently, people commonly judge others in terms of the dialect they speak, and these judgments often (almost always) indicate strains of racial, ethnic, regional, sex, and class biases (Wolfram: 49–60). More simply, based on nothing other than lexicon, syntax, and phonology,

northerners sometimes judge southern speakers to be
"rednecks"; southerners may judge Bostonians to be highly
educated, eastern liberal "snobs"; and many whites (even those
who speak non-standard dialects) judge speakers who grew up
in Harlem (or East LA, Texas, border towns, etc.) to be uneducated and illiterate. Or, as Preston points out, "In the United
States, southern voices awaken stereotypes of racist, barefoot,
poorly educated, Protestant, illegal whiskey drinking, skilled
woodsmen, good ol' boys while urban northern voices strike
some listeners as those of people who are fast-talking, un-
friendly, Jewish or Catholic, time-conscious, impersonal, har-
ried, and dishonest" (94). One example of such sociolinguistic
judgment is easily provided by considering the contrasting attitudes of the American public toward the dialects of John F.
Kennedy and Lyndon Johnson: though obviously more than
language was involved in some of the judgments the public
made about the two men, Kennedy's Harvard-Boston dialect
caused him to be perceived as the more intelligent of the two
(except, of course, by many southerners). But again, Kennedy's
prestige dialect didn't necessarily mean that people *liked* him
better than Johnson: As Preston points out, minority and majority groups often prefer majority groups "for leadership,
responsibility, and competence," but each prefers its own group
"for solidarity and friendliness" (88).

Now, none of this is particularly new to anyone interested in
language study: as long ago as the 1950s and 1960s scholars
like Raven McDavid, Roger Shuy, William Labov, and others
interested in socio- and applied linguistics began to study and
write about the nature and implications of regional dialect differences, language-related bias, etc. During the 1960s there
was an outpouring of fascinating and important books from
the Center for Applied Linguistics and large graduate programs
in socio- and applied linguistics were established.

Unfortunately, the excellent scholarship that has focused on
language bias and dialects has done little to change the general nature of judgment and discrimination that operates in
society where issues of dialect and standard English are concerned. Racism, sexism, and classism—pick your "ism"—man-
age to flourish despite our many efforts to eliminate such vicious and destructive injustices. Walt Wolfram's long interest

in linguistics and dialects causes him to argue against such biases and in favor of celebrating, documenting, and preserving non-standard dialects. Discussing the nature of sociolinguistic bias, Wolfram points to the following irony: "If someone said, 'You're not going to get that job because you're of the wrong gender or of the wrong ethnicity,' they would be in court in one minute. . . . Yet people feel totally free to say, 'You're not going to get that job because you don't talk the way I think you should talk,' whether or not it has anything to do with competency on the job'" (quoted in Flanagan, 1995: 4). In my own experience, I find that language-related prejudice and bias run as deep as (and often alongside of) racism, classism, and sexism. In addition, the linguistic water has become considerably muddier as these kinds of language issues have become debated in relation to written language. Some people, for example, who claim to respect and even enjoy the tremendous variety of oral dialects are deeply offended by and pedagogically worried about students whose spoken dialect "leaks over" into writing. This concern often shows itself in the following kind of statement: "Of course everyone has a right to his/her own dialect, but it is our responsibility as teachers to be sure that students can speak and write in standard English so that they will be able to communicate with the mainstream population and so that they will not be cut off from the possibility of socio-economic mobility." Sometimes this translates more directly into, "I don't care how you talk at home or with your friends, but here [where my dialect is dominant] you will learn to speak correctly [i.e., like me]."

And while I suspect that some people who make this kind of statement really hate non-standard dialects, I also know that many educators make such statements because they are deeply concerned about the kinds of discrimination that non-standard speakers/writers experience in various institutions simply because they are non-standard speakers/writers. That is, one cannot immediately assume that someone making such a statement is operating from a *conscious* position of bias, any more than one can automatically assume that the speaker intends the statement in good faith. Indeed, Lisa Delpit has been variously (mis)understood on the subject as some readers of her work feel that she emphasizes a skills and drills curriculum versus a process approach to teaching writing so that minority students will be able to acquire the language of power. But she clearly argues against worksheet/fill-in-the-blank methods of teaching and is clearly in favor of helping students acquire facility across a range of discourse modes. And she unquestionably respects her students' primary Discourse systems (Delpit, 1988).

Of course, there is also a large contingent of linguistic 'purists' (the Mr. and Ms. Fidditches of languageland), who simply believe that any variation from standard English is evidence of linguistic impropriety—"bad English"—indicating careless, sloppy, irresponsible, lazy (pick your adjective) attitudes toward "proper" English. (If you've not already picked up on the complete picture here, let me simply break it down for you by suggesting that discussions of "correct English," non-standard-dialects, standard English, and essayist literacy often give birth to self-righteous statements from those we might least expect to hold such views. I have heard the most politically and socially liberal of English teachers, even teachers committed to teaching multicultural literatures, openly lament the terrible state into which the language has fallen at the hands—and mouths—of its lower class users.) Another common response to non-standard dialects and education comes from those who believe that the establishment of a power dialect is unfortunate, but there is nothing we can do about it. For example, writing in the *English Journal*, Daniel Heller "regret[s] that the rise of one dialect as the power dialect is generally the result of a history of suppression. Yet, we cannot undo the past" (Heller: 18). (But doesn't such easy acceptance of a wrong condemn us to repeating the oppression of the past?) He also says, "[H]ow or why these particular forms of the language have become the power dialects is not important. What is important is that they are what they are, and our job is to help students enter the public dialogue" (17). Of course, I want students to be able to enter the public dialogue, but "how and why these particular forms of the language have become the power dialects" is terribly important, and students need to become aware of these hows and whys, in order to stop being victimized by them.

Indeed, changing our terminology might help a little in discussing these issues. Given the preceding discussion of standard and non-standard English, I would like to suggest that we stop using the term "non-standard English," and instead, use the more accurate term, "non-dominant." Non-dominant English, then, is the English spoken by the masses of English speakers who have little or no control of the U.S. economy, major institutions, or the people who declare that "broadcast English" is "better" than non-dominant variants.

Over the past 25 years, as the educational establishment has become more and more concerned with "print literacy," and particularly with students' ability to write, these linguistic issues have become part of the dialogue associated with the teaching of writing and reading. For example, if readers read (orally) in their dialect, transforming the marks on the page into their own dialects (and therefore do not read the print exactly as it is printed), are they reading well or poorly? Phonics advocates worry considerably about this kind of reading; people like me or Geneva Smitherman or Constance Weaver (1994) or Frank Smith (1982), who are primarily concerned with readers learning to make meaning of a text, do not worry. Phonics advocates see such readers to be making mistakes; I see them to be doing an admirable job of reading. What I do worry about, however, is the extent to which a non-dominant speaker (reader) may be victimized when the school system perceives the student's dialect to be "incorrect" or "wrong." As I suggested earlier, people who are willing (albeit grudgingly, for many) to tolerate non-dominant dialects in speech often become deeply upset when non-dominant features evidence themselves in the areas we refer to as "print literacy". This is especially true in schools, and even more virulent when non-dominant features show up in students' writing.

Where dialect and standard English are concerned, push usually comes to shove, especially in schools, when *academic* or *essayist literacy* become central issues. For years, it appeared that the primary concerns involved in these "school literacies" focused on particularly marked features of non-dominant dialect that occurred in students' writing. In short, teachers were deeply concerned by students who wrote any of the following: "He ain't got no business doing that." Or, "John, he been sick." Or, "Michael's Momma be sick a lot." Or, "Sheryl walk by here yesterday and take my bicycle." (For a full discussion of the grammar of a non-dominant dialect, see Labov, 1972: *Sociolinguistic Patterns* and *Language in the Inner-City*.) And I repeat that, although most of these examples come from what is often referred to as "Black Dialect" or "Black Vernacular," one's race or skin color have nothing to do with the issue (Wolfram: 55).

What follows, here, is a *very* brief description of some of the linguistic features that characterize Black Vernacular English: I insert these examples to help those readers who have not studied dialects so that you can get a clearer picture of the fact that people who speak non-dominant dialects are not just making lots of mistakes; the differences in their dialects are rule governed—patterns that occur over and over *and* are meaningful. For a much fuller and excellent account of non-dominant dialect features, I recommend Wolfram and Fasold's book, *The Study of Social Dialects in American English*, particularly, chapters 6 and 7. I am focusing on Black Vernacular (or African American Vernacular) for the same reasons that Wolfram and Fasold did: it is one of the more widespread of the non-dominant dialects; because early interest in its origins provoked considerable study of AAVE, we have a considerable body of information on its linguistic characteristics; and it shares features of other non-dominant dialects (Wolfram and Fasold: 31).

Some Examples of African American Vernacular English

I offer only a few phonological examples because most readers are almost certain to have heard the dialect spoken in films and on song recordings, if not in their own community. I purposely use "eye-dialect" spellings here to make it easier on the reader who is not accustomed to phonemic transcription.

STANDARD ENGLISH	AFRICAN AMERICAN VERNACULAR
with—without	wif-wiffout
river	ribber
brother—mother	brotha, brova, bruh, bro—motha, muh
therefore	therefo
kid	keé-id
pin	peé-in
ask	ax

Pluralizations (use of plural markers is optional in AAVE)

desk—desks   des—desses
                          The plural is formed by employ-
                          ing the correct rule of pluralization,
                          but because the non-standard singu-
                          lar ends in "s," the plural is formed
                          by adding "es." This particular ex-
                          ample is relatively common because
                          of the tendency to reduce consonant
                          clusters ("prie*st*" becomes "prie*s*").

policeman—policemen   policeman—policemans, policemens
                          A "regular" pluralization rule is
                      used instead of or along with an
                      irregular.

Third-Person, singular verbs

He goes.   He go.
She says.   She say.

The verb *to be*: This is a particularly interesting feature because
it is so much more complex than most dominant dialect speakers realize. Again, what to many dominant speakers sounds
like random mistakes (because of their ignorance of the grammar of the non-dominant dialect) is really a meaningful gram-
matical pattern.

"My mother is sick."   "My momma, she sick."
                          Copula deletion: No verb to be
                      indicates *present*.

"My mother is almost   "My momma, she be sick."
always sick."   The verb *to be* indicates an
                      ongoing state of affairs—*habitual*.

"My mother was sick a   "My momma, she been sick"
real long time ago"   (a long time ago).
(but she's okay now).   Verb *to be* signals a
                      completed past event.

"My mother was sick, but not as long ago as the woman in the above sentence."	"My momma, she done been sick." Verb *to be* indicates past tense, but not as far past as in the above sentence.

Past Participle

"Nathan walked by here" (yesterday).	"Nathan walk by here" (yesterday). Note that the deletion of the *-ed* follows the same consonant-cluster reduction rule that caused "de*sk*" to become "de*s*". When the word *walked* is spoken, the *-ed* sounds like *-kt*.

Negation

"I never did anything like that."	"I ain't never done nothing like that." A-AVE often uses multiple negation.

As I said above, I provide this very brief sample of some features of Black Vernacular to provide those who are unfamiliar with dialect study a concrete sense of what is being discussed. But it is important to remember that there are other American English dialects that share only a few linguistic characteristics with BV, though their social status is remarkably similar. Chicano English (ChE), for example, "is a variety or dialect of English spoken predominately by bilingual Chicanos and reinforced or reperpetuated as a result of border contact as well as some isolation from some Anglo groups. The bilingual nature of the dialect and the common act of mixing Spanish phrases in with English (code switching within sentences, for example) distinguish it from Black Vernacular and other dialects of English (Penfield and Ornstein-Galicia: 1–2).

But like speakers of BV and other non-dominant dialects, ChE speakers are regularly discriminated against, especially in the southwestern United States where the dialect is perceived as an unsuccessful attempt to speak "correct" English (16). Depending on social class and the region in which one lives, ChE is received differently by Mexican Americans. In urban areas, U.S.-born Chicanos think of Mexican immigrants as Mexicans, as opposed to Chicanos and look down upon the recent immigrants. In border communities, the reverse is true—the new Mexican immigrants have superior status to the Chicanos who have been born in the U.S. border town (21). Indeed, some parents are so sensitive to the fact that those who speak Chicano English are perceived as less intelligent, lower class and so on that they work diligently at forcing their children to lose the "accent." At the same time, many younger speakers of Chicano English view their dialect with pride and try to maintain it (68). But as is so common with non-dominant speakers, educators in general respond negatively to Chicano English, perceiving the speakers to be less intelligent and in need of remediation: they consider ChE to be a "defective form of English which must be wiped out in favor of StE [Standard English]" (72).

Well, as I said above, this is simply a brief "sampler," if you will. And as such, it provides an opportunity to recapitulate some particularly important and, I believe, obvious points that people need to be reminded about in the area of non-dominant dialect or non-dominant English.

1. The fact that given dialects are *non* standard should not suggest that they are in any way inferior to standard dialects.

2. But the very opposition created by the uses of *non* versus *standard*, suggests a second class status for the *non*: i.e., something that is *non* standard, and therefore a deviation from *the* standard is often viewed as less worthy, less good than the standard. Indeed, the word *standard* itself becomes more than a little confusing in these contexts because, in schools, "standards" are something everyone is supposed to *up*hold, measure *up* to: standards are *up* above whatever is *not* standard. And when this meaning of "standard" becomes confused with the meaning intended in discussions of Standard versus non-dominant English, things quickly become even more confused. That is, it is not at all unusual for people to believe that non-domi-

nant dialects do not *measure up to* the standards of "good" (i.e., *standard*) English.

3. It should be self-evident that if people did not believe that non-dominant dialects are inherently inferior, no one would ever have to defend them and schools would not be dedicated to trying to eradicate or change them. In terms of socioeconomic power in our country, it should also be self-evident that, if our major institutions were owned and run by people who spoke/wrote non-dominant varieties of English, what is now non-dominant would suddenly become standard (dominant). (Given socio economic realities, however, I see no immediate threat, regardless of what some of the English First and English Only advocates worry about [Walsh: 101].)

4. And this one is a real kick in the head: no one speaks/ writes perfect standard English (remember, we all have dialects); all of us deviate from the standard at times. But if one is designated as part of the mainstream, part of the power structure, and one's linguistic "deviations" are not those that the dominant Discourse structure most dislikes, then one is speaking/writing standard English. Or to put it more directly, if your deviations from standard English are not associated with being poor, African American, Mexican, Nova Scotian . . . then it's okay. As June Jordan points out, "[W]hite standards of English persist, supreme and unquestioned, in these United States. Despite our multi-lingual population, and despite the deepening Black and white cleavage within that conglomerate, white standards control our official and popular judgments of verbal proficiency and correct, or incorrect, language skills, including speech" (Jordan: 176).

Of course, teachers have long been concerned about matters of dialect, especially what is referred to as "non-standard" dialect. Some have argued, and still argue, that because mainstream society, rightly or wrongly, negatively judges people's ability, intelligence, and class in terms of such non-dominant features, students must learn to eradicate such features from their writing (some still feel the same way about spoken language). And if the argument was not complex enough when it focused primarily on syntax or inflected word endings, over the last 15 years scholars have introduced additional complexities as their studies of non-mainstream students indicates that the issue goes considerably beyond surface-structure features of "correct" usage and grammar. Indeed, the work of Sarah Michaels (1985) and James Gee (1990), and the Scollons (Athabaskan discourse systems) in addition to the work of Robinson on the written discourse systems of Chinese and Japanese people clearly indicates that people have different Discourse systems (both oral and written) that cause them to develop narratives, expositions, arguments in ways markedly different from what is generally expected by those who emphasize "essayist literacy" and "edited American English" in the schools and society at large. And it is toward the issue of Discourse systems that I now wish to turn.

Discourse Systems

Vignettes
Imagine walking up to someone and saying, "You so ugly you look like you daddy beat you mama with a ugly stick." In many situations, the speaker might be suddenly "hit upside the head," but in others, especially if the exchange was taking place between friends in the neighborhood in which I grew up on the southside of Chicago, the other person might quickly reply, "At least my mama got me a daddy. Who beatin' you mama?" Many readers of this book will immediately recognize this as an example of the language game called "the dozens"—a game of insults in which "mamas" often receive considerable ridicule. In its most serious versions, when a game of the dozens becomes real insult, even among friends, someone might get killed. (For an extended description of "sounding" and "the dozens," see Kochman: 52–58.)

I went to a Jesuit high school on the near southside of Chicago, a school known for its academic excellence that somehow managed to attract an unusually mixed clientele. Though the majority of the students were white and affluent, the sons and daughters of judges and politicians (one of Mayor Richard Daley's sons was in attendance), many were from lower and middle class families, a few were people of color. Chicago was then (and still is) a "neighborhood" city of ethnic groups (and proud of it); many of us thought of ourselves as Greeks, or Italians, or Irish, or Polish, or Blacks. The language of those of us who wandered the streets or hung out at city playgrounds was rich, colorful, and non-dominant in varying degrees.

I know that I had heard countless of my classmates call a friend a "sonofabitch" with no problem ensuing. So I was surprised when the following occurred. We were in tenth grade social studies when a Polish classmate jokingly called an Italian classmate a "sonofabitch" because the Italian had grabbed the other guy's pen and thrown it to the back of the room, laughing. It was all in good fun on both sides, and neither of the two had ever engaged in hostility before. But the Italian kid could not allow the Polish kid to call him that specific name, especially in front of other Italians from "the neighborhood" (Chicago's First Ward) because it was an affront to his heritage and, most seriously, to his mother. (Mothers in his particular culture were closely associated with the Madonna.) Desks flew, fists flew, bodies flew, a startled Jesuit screamed, and we pulled Johnny off of the poor Polish guy who never meant anything serious by the remark in the first place.

Of course, I didn't know it then, but I was being introduced to a clash between Discourses.

James Gee differentiates *discourse* with a small *d* and Discourse with a capital *D* as follows: *discourse* is any extended use of language—oral or written narratives, expositions, arguments, articles, and so on. But *Discourse* contains discourses and is "more than just language." Gee offers the following definition: "A *Discourse* is a socially accepted association among ways of using language, of thinking, feeling, believing, valuing, and of acting that can be used to identify oneself as a member of a socially meaningful group or 'social network', or to signal (that one is playing) a socially meaningful 'role'" (Gee, 1990: 142–43). Gee further explains that *dominant Discourses* are those that are used by and provide access to the groups who control the socioeconomic institutions of our society. He further differentiates between *primary Discourses*—those into which we are born and which we acquire by virtue of growing up within a Discourse group—and *secondary Discourses*—those which we acquire as we become interactive over time in various other Discourses (145). Clearly, one's dialect functions powerfully as part of one's primary Discourse.

In discussing the conditions necessary for individuals to establish relative degrees of fluency in secondary Discourses, Gee distinguishes between *Learning* and *Acquisition*. The implications of the distinction are important, complex, and controversial, particularly insofar as we apply them to school activities and various kinds of literacy agendas. For those readers familiar with learning theory, particularly as it is applied to language learning, the distinction is not terribly new, but it is quite important: *acquisition* occurs when an individual is immersed in whatever it is that is being acquired. It involves mistake-making, practice, sometimes a mediator or teacher, but it is essentially a natural process that takes place over time. Likewise, when psycholinguists discuss language-learning, they are almost always thinking in terms of language *acquisition*— that natural process of acquiring language that all human beings in all societies go through and essentially complete by age five, barring brain damage or abuse (Courts, 1991). *Learning* generally refers to a more formal process involving teachers, analytical explanations, and usually "some degree of meta-knowledge" about whatever is being learned (Gee: 146). In terms of language or Discourses, the differentiation might be stated as follows: a person *acquires* a language, acquires Discourses, but *learns* the rules and specific elements that comprise the language or Discourse. Even more simply, we generally *learn about* (meta-knowledge) *that which we have acquired* or are trying to acquire. Indeed, this principle is a fundamental one supporting various "process approaches" used in helping students to become more literate readers and writers.

In terms of print literacy, for example, it is not terribly unusual to find college students—often English majors—who have acquired high degrees of print literacy and are powerful and insightful readers and writers but who cannot consciously cite rules of usage, punctuation, or grammar. While it is sometimes humorously (and accurately) rumored that this is true of some English professors, it is most certainly true of many highly educated people who are excellent readers and writers. Indeed, in the many Writing Across the Curriculum workshops I've taught over the years, I have regularly encountered faculty from other disciplines, faculty members who are much published and highly literate, who were primarily concerned about using writing in their courses because they lacked explicit knowledge about the "rules" of "correct" English. They can identify "mistakes," but cannot explain them. Or in terms of the earlier discussion, they have *acquired* an academic Discourse, but they have not *learned* about all of its aspects.

Some recapitulation may be helpful here: Gee carefully distinguishes between primary and secondary Discourses, pointing out that he is distinctly not talking merely about minor ("trivially different") surface structure differences between nondominant dialects of English and mainstream or standard English. When distinguishing among different primary Discourses, Gee is referring to people who "use language, behavior, values and beliefs to give a different shape to their experience" (151). Consequently, one's primary Discourse must be seen as something more than a world view: it is one's way of shaping a world view and of communicating that world view. These primary Discourses serve as a "'framework' or 'base'" for the secondary Discourses most of us acquire throughout life. Likewise, as people acquire and gain facility with various secondary Discourses, these secondary Discourses influence and change the individual's primary Discourse (You can't go home again), and these changes and modification become a part of the primary Discourse of their children, leading to the "process of historical change of Discourses" (151). We acquire secondary Discourses (Discourses we associate with other major social groups or institutions): that is, the primary Discourse of the home and immediate family is seldom identical to the secondary Discourses we need to be a part of the school or business community.

What is particularly important about Gee's discussion of secondary Discourses are his distinctions between "learning about" versus "acquiring" a secondary Discourse, acquiring full fluency in a secondary Discourse, and the "colonized role" reserved for some within some secondary Discourses. The notion of acquisition versus learning of a Discourse is not a terribly new one and is often discussed in relationship to language: most succinctly put, one can learn about grammar and usage, for example, through study and drill practice. But one's productive *use* of grammar and usage, actual differences in how one uses language, changes only to the extent that one is allowed into the new language community, interactively immersed in the grammar and usage differences, and how much one has the opportunity to use, repeat, make mistakes, correct mistakes, etc. But remember, Gee is talking about considerably more than grammar and usage; he is talking about Discourse systems, ways of shaping and communicating experience, and the ways we are shaped by our own experience.

Next Gee distinguishes between *full fluency* in a Discourse system, a marker of belonging within a given Discourse group, versus anything less than full fluency and *not belonging*: "If you have only partial control over a Discourse, you are not a member of the Discourse; you are an apprentice, an 'outsider', or a 'pretender'" (155). And this last point brings us to Gee's notion of colonization: a colonized individual is a "person internalized by the Discourse as a subordinate, whose very subordination is used as validation for the prestige and power of the Discourse" (155). By way of exemplification, consider the college English professor who attempts to enter the Discourse of the local farmers: if the professor has had some experience with their Discourse, they may allow him into the dialogue, but it will always be clear that the professor has been "allowed" in, a clear subordinate; if he has no experience with the Discourse, has had no chance to acquire any of its defining features, he is likely to meet with either silence or mockery. Of course, professors and teachers often do the same to people who have not had the opportunity to become fully fluent in the school or academic Discourse.

One important difference, however, is to consider the fact that the farmers have not been assigned the role of helping that professor acquire their Discourse. But isn't that exactly the role of the teacher? To help others acquire the Discourse of the school or of a discipline? More common examples abound for most English teachers who have had the opportunity of reading student papers or hearing oral presentations in which the speaker/writer is "trying to sound the ways s/he thinks smart folks are supposed to sound." The resulting overformalization often leads to convoluted sentences and malapropisms. And in the process of making the colonized role of the speaker/writer clear to all concerned, teachers often make lists of such "mistakes" and put them up on bulletin boards in teachers' lounges so everyone can have a little laugh at the expense of the outsider who is less than fluent in the dominant Discourse. I might add, here, that I don't think that this kind of thing indicates intentional meanness on the part of the teachers as much as it indicates a genuine lack of understanding of how dominant their own Discourse system is and how difficult it can be for learners to gain fluency in that Discourse.

Michel Foucault, discussing something similar to what I've been discussing above, writes of "fellowships of discourse" ("The Discourse on Language": 225—*DL* in future references). It is the function of this fellowship "to preserve or to reproduce discourse, but in order that it should circulate within a closed community, according to strict regulations, without those in possession being dispossessed by this very distribution" (*DL*: 225). Although Foucault says that "few such 'fellowships of discourse' remain," I don't think I'm doing violence to his ideas by suggesting that many such fellowships exist, but they are less clearly defined than those to which Foucault refers when he mentions technical, medical, scientific, and economic discourse groups (*DL*: 226). Many readers of this book may already be thinking of examples in their own lives as they attempted to acquire a secondary Discourse only to realize, at some crucial moment, that they were still novices. But let me interject a few examples growing out of my own experience. With few exceptions, most of this book is written in standard English and I am relying on a secondary Discourse I acquired over my 30 years of experience in academia. In a few parts of the book, I write in non-dominant *dialect*, but seldom (at least not intentionally) do I stray from academic Discourse (well, at least not too often). Having grown up in a consciously standard-English household, I acquired a highly "standard," white, middle-class Discourse system. But many of my peers, most of whom cared little about standard English or essayist literacy, helped me "overcome" my home upbringing and through them I acquired many non-dominant features and a Discourse system rather different than that of my socially conscious parents. Of course, I was not at all conscious of all of this and moved between the different Discourse systems with ease. In the home, "damn" and "hell" were the only "bad" words I ever remember hearing. Outside the home, I could use "fuck" and "motherfucker" as well as anyone in the group, often getting those words or variations of them to precede or follow almost every noun in a given sentence. Many of us in the group inserted variations of these words in between syllables of other words: i.e., "fanfuckingtastic," "unfuckingbelievable." I suspect that more than a few readers of this book are fully familiar with such language.

My lack of consciousness of my own Discourse switches was brought to my attention one time following an English Department meeting. The socio/applied linguist Dennis Preston, then my colleague, mentioned to me that he had seldom heard anyone speak so differently in a formal meeting as opposed to informal situations as I apparently did. As we talked about it a little, because I had never really thought about it, I realized that I was probably trying to hide that kid who grew up on the southside of Chicago in city playgrounds and streets. Because I wanted to be accepted by the "real" professionals, I was apparently overformalizing. This incident with Preston further reminded me of an incident that had occurred to me as an undergraduate in one of Dr. Virginia McDavid's linguistics classes. As she returned a paper I had written she asked me if I intended to be a lawyer. Responding "no," I asked why she had thought so. She told me, gently and with a smile on her face, that she had seldom seen language used so formally and effectively to obscure meaning except in law briefs. On reviewing the paper, I realized that almost every sentence began with something like, "It should be further noted that in consequence of this event . . . ." A reverse example occurred when I overheard a colleague from another discipline cursing a blue streak in the gym. The only problem was that he pronounced the words too carefully and put them in the wrong places. He knew the lexicon, but had not acquired the Discourse at all. I wanted to tell him that he really shouldn't swear in public until he learned how to do it correctly. (Even I have my language biases!)

A second major point that Gee makes is that primary Discourses "can never give rise to *liberating literacies*" (156). This is in no way to diminish or demean the primary Discourse: It is simply to point out that without meta-knowledge about the primary Discourse, I cannot critique it because I am entirely contained by it. Indeed, without specifically saying so Gee raises one of the most serious problems in language study, especially in the areas of socio- and applied linguistics: we must use language in order to study language; the only way we can examine the "thing" is to use the thing itself. (Hermeneutically sealed, so to speak?) The point strikes me as particularly important because it suggests that classrooms should not only be places in which students become *conscious* users of their primary Discourses and are encouraged and assisted in the acquisition of secondary Discourses, but they must also be places in which primary *and* secondary Discourses are analyzed so that students can learn to critique and become conscious of the Discourses that contain them, to the extent that is possible. And Gee's point that we fail both mainstream and non-mainstream students in this area is worth noting.

It is also important to remember that, especially for non-mainstream students, there is likely to be considerable tension between the primary Discourse and the *politics* of acquiring a secondary Discourse, especially one that is characteristic of the dominant, white power structure. The acquisition of the secondary Discourse, in this case, threatens the sense of identity associated with the primary Discourse, particularly insofar as the acquisition of the secondary Discourse modifies the primary Discourse: in a sense, particularly given the facts of racism, classism, and sexism in our society, we are asking the learner to give up the sense of identity and belonging guaranteed through the primary Discourse in order to attain a colonized position in the secondary Discourse. A tough choice, to say the least.

As Foucault points out,

Education may well be, as of right, the instrument whereby every individual, in a society like our own, can gain access to any kind of discourse. But we well know that in its distribution, in what it permits and in what it prevents, it follows the well-trodden battle-lines of social conflict. Every educational system is a political means of maintaining or of modifying the appropriations of discourse, with the knowledge and powers it carries with it. (*DL*: 227)

And none of this offers easy answers for teachers or anyone else. Students and teachers are likely to find themselves in one of several complex positions related to the entire issue of celebrating primary Discourses and acquiring secondary Discourses. Teachers who encourage students to use and examine their primary Discourses are quite likely to be accused of trying to limit the students from ever gaining access to the dominant Discourse. Teachers who encourage the acquisition of secondary Discourses may be accused of trying to erase the identity of the students as expressed through the primary Discourse. Parents and teachers, trying to force students into using a dominant secondary Discourse may cause so much resistance among the students that they consciously resist any change. Or, students, trying to please parents and teachers may gain facility with a dominant secondary Discourse and simultaneously *acquire* all of the prejudices that are part of that dominant Discourse. No matter how we look at it, Discourse and self-identity are inextricably intertwined.

The Problem of Changing Identity

Emphasizing her own linguistic identity, Gloria Anzaldúa writes:

> So, if you really want to hurt me, talk badly about my language. Ethnic identity is twin skin to linguistic identity—I am my language. Until I can take pride in my language, I cannot take pride in myself. Until I can accept as legitimate Chicano Texas Spanish, Tex-Mex and all the other languages I speak, I cannot accept the legitimacy of myself. . . . and as long as I have to accommodate the English speakers rather than having them accommodate me, my tongue will be illegitimate.
>
> I will no longer be made to feel ashamed of existing. I will have my voice: Indian, Spanish, white. I will have my serpent's tongue—my woman's voice, my sexual voice, my poet's voice. I will overcome the tradition of silence. (59)

As should be clear by now, dialects and Discourses, language issues in general, are highly political issues. But as Anzaldúa so clearly states, one's language is also closely tied to one's sense of identity, and the pressure schools and society put on people to change their language can be an assault on their identity. In his book, *The End of Education*, William Spanos discusses the treatment of minority students in higher education with respect to their language. He observes that the "immediate and essential purpose" of many programs (like Educational Opportunities Programs) designed to "help" minorities obtain college educations was "to teach them [minority students] to speak and write standard English." He goes on to say that, "Such 'liberal' programs . . . were finally intended to annul as much as possible the linguistic difference endemic to the life of African-Americans, Hispanics, and other ethnic minorities . . . and thus to induce them to take their *proper* place in the dominant culture and sociopolitical order—the white world" (184). He further suggests that, "The essential—because 'naturally' given—assumption informing the raison d'etre is of the traditional humanist university, the repository of the mature fruits of civilization, is that it constitutes a site offering the uncultivated or 'ignorant' individual student an 'opportunity' for 'self-fulfillment.' As a consequence of this assumption, students, especially minority students hitherto denied the opportunity of higher education—are expected to feel grateful to the liberal society that in its knowing largesse offers them such an opportunity to achieve fruition (and they largely do)" (199).

And while I fully agree with Spanos's comments, I also believe that the pressures applied to individuals in these matters of language and identity begin to occur well before they reach college. As John Ogbu points out: "Specifically, blacks and similar minorities (e.g., American Indians) believe that in order for a minority person to succeed in school academically, he or she must learn to think and act white. . . . That is, striving for academic success is a subtractive process: the individual black student following school standard practices that lead to academic success is perceived as . . . 'acting white' with the inevitable outcome of losing his or her black identity, abandoning black people and black causes, and joining the enemy, namely, white people" (Ogbu, 1987; see also, Ogbu, 1978).

The accuracy of Ogbu's observation is exemplified in Victor Villanueva's experience. He speaks of the pressure and tension he felt as he was pushed toward learning standard English and the sense of "alienation" that accompanied the process. He felt as though he had been "pushed into racelessness" by both his father and his schooling as he "chooses" to master the dominant Discourse: He is fully aware that he is not "fully adopted by the white community," at the same time that he loses "kinship" with his own community (40). A Chicano American, Manuel Ramirez III, speaks of the kind of no-man's-land experienced by some of his people:

> Those of us who have lived in the border area of South Texas, where my hometown, Roma, is located, sometimes jokingly refer to ourselves as the people that General Santa Ana sold to the United States at the end of the U.S. Mexico War during the 19th century. At any rate, as Mexican Americans, we often find ourselves caught in the various types of ethnic dilemmas. Our friends and relatives in Mexico call us "pochos," while some Anglos do not accept us. Sometimes we feel like a people without a country. (Ramirez: 100)

And Simon Ortiz writes eloquently of the forces that operate to erase the sense of *kinship* that Villanueva mentions when he discusses his own experiences as he moves away from his life as an Acoma Indian and into the world of the dominant society: "This is not an unusual phenomenon, as anyone from a colonized people can say. This phenomenon is why heritage, culture, even native languages, and identity are ignored, forgotten, and lost. It is not by choice that it takes place; it is literally by force that it happens. Native American people have experienced it since the so-called 'discovery' of the New World as they've run the gauntlet of genocide and enslavement, Manifest Destiny, U.S. citizenship, and assimilation" (20).

But perhaps the problems associated with identity need not be so immense and immutable. To ameliorate the problem, teachers must help students become much more critically conscious of the nature of Discourse systems, the pressure brought to bear by the dominant Discourse to erase Discourses of difference, and the choices that surround the acquisition of secondary Discourses.

It is a truism for all of us that, as we learn and grow, we change. The more radical that learning is, the more it conflicts with past beliefs and practices, the more we change and the more likely we are to be in conflict with the group with whom we previously identified. Most of the readers of this particular text, for example, know that they can't go home again, partly because none of us are the same individuals we used to be, and partly because the world of home does not particularly welcome the kinds of people we have become, precisely because the changes we have gone through put us at odds with practices and beliefs that make home what it is. Of course, depending on the nature of "home," many of us can physically go back, and because people are often polite, those who stayed at home sometimes play a pretending game that allows all of us to get through a visit or a holiday. For others, homecomings can be considerably more painful. But no matter how you look at it, home has changed and so have we.

I am reminded of a first-year college student I taught, an African American female from an all African American area of Detroit. Bright, reasonably self-confident, and articulate (in oral non-dominant English and relatively standard written English), she thrived in college. She happily interacted with other black students from the Detroit area, and she also enjoyed new relationships with the much larger population of white, middle-class students. But her journal entries describing her first visit home after two months in this new middle to upper-middle class environment were disturbing because they so clearly indicated her own upset. Her journal described the encounter she had with her grandmother, apparently within less than 30 minutes after she had entered the apartment. Though the journal entry was not clear about the topic under discussion, it sounded like her grandmother had asked her how she "like that college," and her answer disturbed the grandmother who was quoted in the journal as accusing the girl of becoming "uppity," and was told that unless she wanted to be "smacked upside the head," she had better remember where she "come from and who her people be." As a teacher interested in dialect, I first thought the problem was related to changes in the girl's oral dialect, but on reflection, I knew that couldn't be the case. Though there had been some surface structure change, there hadn't been that much. Consequently, on reflection, I have to assume that the change went deeper than dialectal surface structures. Lest this seem oversimplified, let me also point out that one of the changes she was undergoing was a powerful move toward becoming more politically active. And I suspect that her identity was changing and growing in some important ways that, perhaps, challenged the values and actions of her "home" and the people associated with home. She and I talked about the issue at some length and she pretty much convinced me that she could negotiate the problem on her own. Not that it really mattered, however, because she was clearly going her own way and I didn't have much to say one way or the other.

But the point here is this. This girl was articulate, bright, and self confident. Furthermore, her journal writing indicated a high degree of consciousness of what was happening to her. I did not then, nor do I think now that we need to worry too much about "identity changes" in someone like this.

But what about students for whom the process might not be as conscious. In a very real sense, the earlier students are moved into language activities that genuinely engage them in authentic uses of language across primary *and* secondary Discourse systems, the more likely they are to not even notice that choices are being made and that they are acquiring new identities. While I am a little concerned about this, I suspect that an overt confrontation and explanation of what is really going on, a discussion that involves students as equal participants in an examination of what it is they are doing in classrooms might not only be healthy and helpful in regards to making choices about identity changes, but equally important, it would change the nature of schooling by indicating that students should be given the opportunity to play an integral role in their own learning. Students who are consciously making choices might be among the most powerful learners we could ever encounter. And this is one of James Gee's important points in his discussions of primary and secondary Discourse systems: he insists that meta-knowledge is essential for the individual to be able to use any Discourse system in a liberating way.

He is, of course, correct: consciousness is everything.

Chapter 3

Real People/Real Stories: Voices from the Margin

"Sometimes I two-time think. . . . I think like in my family and in my house. And then I think like in school and other places. Then I talk. They aren't the same, you know." (A five-year-old, bilingual Puerto Rican child quoted in Walsh: vii)

Learning to listen to different voices, hearing different speech challenges the notion that we must all assimilate—share a single similar talk—in educational institutions. . . . It is important for those of us who are Black, who speak in particular patois as well as standard English, to express ourselves in both ways. (Hooks, 1989: 79–80)

When will a legitimately American language, a language including Nebraska, Harlem, New Mexico, Oregon, Puerto Rico, Alabama and working-class life and freeways and Pac-Man become the language studied and written and glorified in the classroom. (Jordan: 128)

Readers of this chapter may have to "two-time think." In fact, it might be good for all of us to learn to do so instead of simply expecting those who are locked out of the mainstream to learn to do so. And we also must heed Hooks's point that we need "as many languages on hand as we can know or learn" (Hooks, 1989: 79). For teachers of language and literacy, this new agenda, one that does not simply intend to eradicate nondominant dialects and Discourses and replace them with the "standard," means that teachers themselves must know more about various Discourses and dialects. This chapter begins with a look at some of the important research that has been done over the past 20 years on some specifically different ways various groups of people use to organize and develop their narratives (expositions, arguments). I will present several cases involving students whose Discourse systems are different from those of the school, and because of that difference cause both students and teachers a variety of problems. In part, the discussion will focus on the kinds of bias and discrimination that come into play when dominant, mainstream institutions make judgments about the intelligence and quality of students' speaking and writing (hearing, reading, and thinking) abilities based on misinformation, prejudice, and often ignorance with regard to important aspects of socio- and applied linguistics. More specifically, I intend to examine the roles that schools and teachers play as they (mis)shape the discourse structures (and lives) of the minority and foreign students who populate classrooms from kindergarten through graduate school. In addition, this chapter also explores some of the complexities facing teachers who work with such students.

James Collins examines differences in narrative structures among some culturally different groups of people, focusing on differences among groups and also differences between oral and written narrative (57). He points out that someone who has grown up within a primarily oral culture is likely to rely on the structure of oral narrative as s/he begins to try to produce written narratives. Noting the research on American Indians, African Americans, Hawaiian Americans, working-class British, and even North American communities whose narratives evidence the influence of oral cultures, he points out that: "Oral narratives are much more likely to have a loose episodic structure, with an underlying schema provided by implicit symbolic contrasts and thematic relations, but often with no explicit connections between parts of the narrative. Written narratives, conversely, having the considered quality, the mulling-over which is possible with writing, tend to have more tightly articulated plots with explicit lexical and syntactic connections made between parts of the overall account. All discourse presumes a context, a frame of reference, but written narratives are not tied to an immediate context of speaking and their audience is always raised first in imagination (however accurately). Hence, written narratives tend to have a more decontextualized quality than their oral counterparts: they replace, for example, the richness of intonation and gesture with a search for lexical precision and syntactic flexibility" (59). (Unless, of course, one's writing is patterned after one's primary, oral Discourse.)

In their very well-known book *Narrative, Literacy and Face in Interethnic Communication* Ronald and Suzanne Scollon differentiate between oral literacy and "essayist literacy" in which "the important relationships to be signaled are those between sentence and sentence, not those between speakers, not those between sentence and speaker." And they note that the reader of such a work exists in a "third-person relationship to the author and this consistent maintenance of the point of view is one of the hallmarks of written text" (48). What is clear from their discussion of the Athabaskan people, as they are contrasted with mainstream Canadians or Americans, is the obvious fact that their Discourse system reflects a set of cultural schema, a world view that is partly evidenced in their Discourse systems. In his discussion of the Scollons's work, James Gee points out that: (1) The Athabaskans place a premium on their own and others' sense of individuality and "prefer to avoid conversation except when the point of view of all participants is well known" (Gee, 1990: 62). Middle and upper-middle class Americans, on the other hand, often delight in employing conversation as a means to find out the points of view of other people. (2) Athabaskan children (subordinates) are expected to observe their superiors (parents) who, as superiors, demonstrate the values and ways of acting that the children should emulate. Mainstream American children, on the other hand are praised for their precociousness: the more articulate and forward they are in conversations with adults, the brighter they are perceived to be. (3) Middle and upper-middle class Americans often "blow their own horns," so to speak, feeling it appropriate to project a positive sense of self and a positive sense of what the future holds for oneself. But Athabaskans find it inappropriate to speak highly of one's self, and even dangerous to predict good luck. Gee goes on to point out that, "The Scollons list many other differences, including differences in systems of pausing that ensure that English speakers select most of the topics and do most of the talking in an interethnic encounter. The net result of these communication problems is that each group ethnically stereotypes the other. The English speaker comes to believe that the Athabaskan is unsure, aimless, incompetent, and withdrawn. The Athabaskan comes to believe that the English speaker is boastful of his abilities, sure he can predict the future, careless with luck and far too talkative" (Gee, 1990: 62–3). And while it is clearly important to note that "each group ethnically stereotypes the other," it is equally important to note that, in an American public school, the Athabaskan student would be expected to measure up to the "superior" American Discourse system.

Another example of Discourse difference, one considerably closer to Main Street USA, is provided by Shirley Brice Heath's well-known book *Ways with Words: Language, Life, and Work in Communities and Classrooms.* Heath's work focuses on language and literacy development in two communities. The community she names Roadville is essentially white; the other, Tracton, is essentially African American. Both groups are employed as mill workers. Roadville mothers spend considerable amounts of time interacting with their children, are directive and prescriptive in terms of teaching their children language, and feel responsible for teaching their children how to talk "correctly," how to read, and how to behave, all in preparation for good school behavior. Although their background is somewhat more directive than may be typical of middle-class white households, Roadville children grow up in a Discourse that closely parallels what will be expected of them when they reach school (which, I might add, does not constitute a complement for what schools expect).

For the Tracton children, the story is different. Babies in this group are seldom isolated in cribs or playpens, are regularly passed around from lap to lap, are surrounded by language but seldom addressed directly during their first six months. In this community, interactions are highly communal, storytelling is common and involves considerable embellishment, children are not often read to and reading alone is considered anti-social. The children do learn to read before school, but most of the reading involves food labels, names of cars, and reading directions: "Reading is almost always set within a context of immediate action" (191–192). In short, although they are print literate and good storytellers, the Tracton children's highly interactive, communal Discourse differs considerably from what they will experience when they get to school.

In a very different kind of study, James Robinson's work in contrastive rhetoric reveals aspects of Discourse differences among East Asians. Relying in part on the work of a graduate student, Gu Hui Yun, he discusses some of the rhetorical approaches that these East Asians are taught to use in their writing. To "draw the dragon," for example, directs the writer to emulate the ancient artist who would begin at the end, so to speak, with the dragon's tail, and then move body, legs, arms, eventually the head, and finally the eyes, thus giving life to the dragon. If the dragon is drawn well, once the life giving eye has been added, it will fly away, complete unto itself. He also discusses another rhetorical pattern, the ki-shou-ten-ketsu pattern: beginning with a topical statement (ki), the second part (shou) adds defining detail about the topic. The third part (ten) appears to digress by offering apparently unrelated information. And the final part (ketsu) provides a strong ending that pulls everything together (see also, Young: 99, 132–135).

Along these same lines, Carolyn Matalene and Guanjun Cai, in two separate articles, discuss the inductive nature of East Asian writing and the fact that a straightforward statement of theme is a sign of disrespect. These authors also mention the heavy reliance on quotes and references to the past used by the East Asian students, an approach that emphasizes the importance of the great voices of the past and diminishes the personal voice/views of the author.

While a discussion of East Asian rhetorical practices may, at first, seem somewhat divorced from what I've been discussing, a little further exploration may make its relevance clearer. Still exploring the challenge of teaching East Asian students, Ronald Scollon adds to the discussion.

Ronald Scollon writes about his experiences teaching students at Ching Yi University in Shalu, Taiwan—they are distinctly *not* learning English composition in a language environment surrounding them with native English speakers. Nevertheless, the example serves to further illustrate some of the complex issues involved when one group is asked to fit into the Discourse system of another, particularly when the teacher needs more information about the students' primary Discourse (R. Scollon, 1991). Scollon relates how he tried to follow the suggestions of Peter Elbow and many other teachers of writing who emphasize the importance of writers establishing an individual voice. Following the leads of people like Ken

Macrorie, Elbow, and many others, Scollon set about having his Chinese students engage in the process of "freewriting" in order to lead them into the writing of personal narrative. Such a path, often used in writing courses in America these days, would lead the students to "express the self," and thereby come to a fuller understanding of self. But his students found the approach "almost completely unintelligible" (1). As Scollon comes to more fully understand the influence of Confucianism on his students (and almost certainly Buddhism, though Scollon doesn't mention it), he realizes that the emphasis on self-expression at the center of his writing approach poses a genuine threat to the students' sense of self: "In this *Confucian or Chinese sense of self, one is more a self in human relationships, and less a self in isolation*" (2). In traditional Buddhism, those who seek "the way" are expected to *lose self*, not go around trying to discover or assert it. And even given the explicit attacks on Confucianism in Communist China, Chinese Communism emphasizes the absolute subordination of the individual to the society.

Scollon goes on to discuss the structure of the *Pa Ku Wen* (also *ba gu wen*), also known as the "eight-legged essay" (8). Noting that this traditional structure for writing essays was established in 1386 and de-emphasized in 1898 when the government civil-service exams were discontinued, Scollon resists the argument that it no longer influences Chinese students. He argues that any essay form that held such sway would not simply disappear as an influence on contemporary Chinese. I was fortunate enough to have the opportunity to discuss Scollon's paper and this issue with a visiting Chinese linguist who was on sabbatical from her position as a teacher of Chinese in a Japanese university.[1] She supported Scollon's position by explaining that, although the *Pa Ku Wen* is no longer formally taught, many of its underlying principles continue to inform the essay structure (modes of thinking) that contemporary Chinese are taught. As we continued to discuss the issues involved here, I asked her about the potential problem of asking Chinese or Japanese students to write personal narratives "expressions of self," and she immediately supported Scollon's point that such a demand would cause genuine problems for

1. For political reasons, this individual asked that her name not be used.

such students: first, because a prominent teacher had asked them to do it, and to avoid complying would involve the students in consciously insulting the older, legitimate authority figure; second, complying with such a demand represented a violation of a community tradition of subordinating self to the network of community relationships that are at the center of the society.

At this point the conversation became particularly interesting because she had also been sitting in on a graduate course I was teaching in "Whole Language Approaches to Teaching Multicultural Literatures." After about three weeks of becoming acclimated and coming to feel a reasonable degree of comfort in the classroom, she began to participate in class discussions and activities. When the class turned to Chinese culture in China and in America, working with Maxine Hong Kingston's *Woman Warrior,* this scholar regularly began to share personal experiences of her own including telling some personal stories about political/religious disagreements between her and her mother. (Although she never *wrote* any of these narratives, I have reasons to suspect that she was more concerned about potential political recrimination than about revelation of self. Just as the *Pa Ku Wen* influences students long after its formal demise, so also does the memory of the now defunct Red Guard.) At any rate, in a private conversation, I was able to ask her how she would be treated when she returned to China, given that she was becoming somewhat accustomed to engaging in (or to pretending to engage in?) "expressions of self." Her reply was fascinating on two counts: first, she told me that she would be much more hesitant to tell personal stories of any kind when she returned to the mainland because it would offend her people; second, she said that her status as a scholar who had studied in both China *and* the United States would be such that most people would hesitate to criticize her. (So classism, educational elitism, and attendant hostilities are as alive and well in The People's Republic as they are here!)

A Necessary Digression

Up to this point in this chapter, I have been trying to loosely imitate certain structural elements central to the *Pa Ku Wen,* without, unfortunately, any of the facility of a practiced Chinese writer. In fact, the more I tried, the more confused I got (which is probably self-evident). I began the chapter with quotations, made explicit reference to the content of the quotations, moved then to ("Voice of the Sage") by relying on the work of Collins, the Scollons, Robinson, and Gee. Slowly, in the discussion of experiences with the Chinese scholar, I began to insert my own voice (in parentheses). And still I have not gotten to the main point of the chapter.

If I were to continue to be as faithful to the structure of the *Pa Ku Wen* as my meager skill might allow, I would continue in two following paragraphs to present my main point, albeit in an indirect manner relying on extended metaphor as much as possible, eventually present my main point directly and finish with what is "less than a conclusion than a leaving behind of impressions" (R. Scollon, 9). But as I have already pointed out, I have not the skill to emulate the masters of this Discourse and already risk humiliation in the attempt. While I have reason to hope that my readers will excuse the weakness of this attempt, I suspect that if it were marked with stigmatizing linguistic features associated with speakers of non-dominant dialects or second language learners my readers would not be as forgiving as I hope them to be.

The simple fact is that, without considerably more direction and practice, I am unable to function successfully within the foreign Discourse. My past immersion in Western essayist literacy consistently forces me into a relatively traditional academic kind of writing.

My Turn

As the work of Collins, the Scollons, Heath, and Gee suggests, different groups of people who grow up in different cultures do not only have different dialects (and languages) but they also have different ways of telling the stories of who they are and what they think. And the dominant institutions of the United States, particularly the schools, discriminate against both the oral and written Discourse systems of people who do not participate in the primary Discourse represented by the educated middle and upper-middle class in the United States. Turning the tables, so to speak, on those who represent the dominant Discourse in the United States, the African American writer June Jordan criticizes the impersonal and irresponsible Discourse of those in power and tells the story of an attempt to help some of her college student recapture the power and glory of their own Discourse. In her essay, "Problems of Language in a Democratic State" (126–134), Jordan agrees that many students, minority and otherwise, are not good readers/ writers, critical thinkers, but she notes that both black kids and whites ("who fared only somewhat better" 127–128) were often victims of schools that cared little about "their language, their style, their sense of humor, their ideas of smart, their music, their need for a valid history and a valid literature—history and literature that included their faces and their voices" (128). Jordan focuses on the empty content, the irresponsible language that characterizes the language of the powerful as they fence with one another on Sunday "news" talk shows, carefully using the passive voice whenever responsibility for a position might cause them a problem; she characterizes this language as something that has been "homogenized into an official 'English' language that can only express non-events involving nobody responsible, or lies. If we lived in a democratic State our language would have to hurtle, fly, curse, and sing, in all the common American names, all the undeniable and representative and participating voices of everybody here" (129). While she focuses on the Nixon administration's descriptions of massive air attacks on Vietnam as "unselfish missions" (32), it might be more appropriate in the 1990s to look back at the rhetoric of the Kennedy/Johnson administrations from the perspective now offered by Robert McNamara's book about how wrong the entire Vietnam fiasco was. But regardless of the examples one uses, Jordan's suggestion that we eliminate the passive voice is an interesting one. On the other hand, mandating changes in language practices simply doesn't work. And even if we could eliminate the passive voice, it wouldn't have stopped those who made up lies about dominoes and the invasion of California by the North Vietnamese army. Nor will it do any good for the dead Americans and Vietnamese.

In another essay, "Nobody Mean More to Me Than You and the Future Life of Willie Jordan," June Jordan discusses her experience as a teacher of a course focusing on helping students recapture the power of their primary Discourse (Black

Vernacular) and helping them to learn to write in the dialect. It is here that Jordan discusses the features of this Discourse somewhat differently from the discussions that characterize academic sociolinguistic descriptions of dialect. I particularly like her four initial rules: (1) *"Black English is about a whole lot more than mothafuckin"*; (2) *"If it's wrong in Standard English it's probably right in Black English, or, at least, you're hot"*; (3) *"If it don't sound like something that come out somebody mouth then it don't sound right. If it don't sound right then it ain't hardly right. Period"*; and (4) *"Forget about the spelling. Let the syntax carry you"* (179–180). She goes on, importantly, to emphasize the implicitly oral nature of the Discourse, the absolute centrality of human beings involved in communicating with one another, and the fact that, by definition, call-and-response Discourse demands communicative *interaction* rather than the distanced, impersonal prose that characterizes essayist literacy. And yet, an essay that begins with hope and excitement leaves the reader as angry as Jordan and her students. Daring to use their recaptured Discourse, these students attempt to protest the death of a brother of one of their classmates: Willie Jordan's unarmed brother, Reggie, had been shot to death by New York police. Of course, no one would print their non-dominant letters or carry these non-dominant voices on television. Likewise, Willie's own letter, a powerful piece written in standard English receives no response. The lesson, for me, is this: the dominant Discourse in any society has the power to bury the non-dominant voices (and bodies) of those who do not share that Discourse. It can send them to kill and be killed in a senseless war; it can marginalize them socially and economically assuring that they will be dismissed as lazy, ignorant fools and troublemakers. That this fact is true of many societies, certainly not just the United States, makes the struggle all the more difficult and all the more important.

Real People/Real Experiences

June Jordan's focus on her students, Willie in particular, moves this discussion from generalizations to specifics. And what follows is a description/analysis of two case studies of students whose primary Discourses differed from those of their teachers and the institution and one case study of a teacher's attempt to help a mother and her son attain print literacy.

Sarah Michaels presents us with a description of some language experiences of two elementary school students (Michaels, 1985). The first student, Deena, is a first-grader participating in "sharing time"—the daily oral monologues students proudly present to the entire class. Anyone familiar with this fairly common school ritual knows that it is usually an important time for the speakers who have an opportunity to "share" some recent, significant element or event in their lives. It is an important social and linguistic event because the speakers are sometimes operating in a linguistically authentic moment—they are telling something that they actually want to share—and they have a real and usually interested audience. Of course, as with any school event, it is relatively easy to turn the authentic moment into an inauthentic one in which the student is simply trying (or supposed to be trying) to evidence that s/he has mastered some skill the teacher expects the student to master. In this case, Deena makes the mistake of thinking that the moment contains the possibility for authentic sharing, not realizing that the teacher is using the moment to "teach" Deena to *focus* on and *develop* a *single* point without digression. And just as Deena does not understand the teacher's agenda, neither does the teacher understand Deena's Discourse system, a system that relies on associational elements in a story to dramatize the reason for telling the story in the first place.

The teacher, "Mrs. Jones," described Deena's sharing-time talk as "'long, rambling, moving from one thing to the next.' She saw this as a problem of planning, saying that Deena was always 'talking off the top of her head' and simply didn't take time to 'plan what she wanted to say in advance.'" In an attempt to prevent such rambling, Mrs. Jones told Deena "to share one thing that's very important, one thing" (37).

Unfortunately for Deena, her "complex development of a theme through a series of related episodes," which "allows for shifts in time, place, or characters across major episode boundaries" violates the focus on "one thing" demanded by the teacher. In short, because the teacher does not share a knowledge of Deena's narrative (Discourse) system, the teacher perceives disconnected, unplanned rambling. Deena, of course, has no idea why the teacher doesn't see the obvious connections in her story (41). This is, after all, the way her primary, home Discourse operates; indeed, in Deena's primary Discourse system, it would not be at all unusual for listeners who knew anything about the events she was sharing to actively participate, interrupting and adding in order to help embellish the story.

But because the teacher does not know about different Discourse structures, she perceives Deena to be somewhat obstinately ignoring the directions (to focus on one thing). Consequently, she interrupts Deena's sharing, attempting to get Deena to "focus," and this causes Deena to become upset and discouraged: "Sharing time got on my nerves. She was always interruptin' me, sayin' 'that's not *important enough*,' and I hadn't hardly started talking!" (41). Aside from the fact that Deena's statement here indicates her understandable frustration, it also indicates ("I hadn't hardly started talking!") that this story was important to Deena and she *clearly had a plan* to tell her full story. It also indicates how very early in the educational system teachers feel free (perhaps even duty bound) to take control of the students' stories—how very early it is made clear to students that it is not *what* you have to say that counts, but *how* you say it.

Michaels points out that the teacher and student are at "cross purposes. Mrs. Jones was looking for simple, prose-like description similar to that in the preamble on a single topic, organized in such a way that it sounded 'important.' Deena, however, intended to develop the theme of her new coat through a series of personal narrative accounts, as if to highlight the importance of her new coat by showing its reflection in the experience of key family members" (42). Indeed, Deena thinks that the teacher's interruptions, her attempt to keep Deena talking about only *one thing*, were intended to get her (Deena) to say more about the episode she was developing at the time. Regardless of how one might sympathize with either the teacher or Deena, it is important to note that while the teacher is frustrated, she is not victimized, but Deena is; the teacher is, after all, in control, in power. Unfortunately, instead of learning anything about a new Discourse system or a new way of telling a story, Deena simply begins to learn that in the Discourse of the school, neither she nor her experiences count. It is also most important to note that the teacher is not trying to hurt Deena in any way—her intentions may be misguided, but they are still well intended. On the other hand, good intentions seldom heal a wound.

Following her discussions of Deena's experience, Michaels goes on to describe the experience of a sixth grade Hispanic boy in Boston—a boy described by his teacher as "'the classroom bully' due to personal problems he was having at home" (44). Michaels describes both the boy's experience as he writes (on a word processor) about his experience on a class trip to the circus as well as the direction he receives from the teacher as she involves him in her version of the writing *process*. While the description serves (sadly), in part, to exemplify *how not to* conference with a student and how to use intervention in a writer's process to guarantee that the process will result in empty prose, it further exemplifies how destructive a teacher can be when s/he does not understand how to engage the speaker/author in the development of his/her own story. In brief, because the teacher does not understand some of the rather sophisticated content and connections Elliott creates in his story, and because, in fact, she is more interested in having him develop a nice, little "school paragraph," she edits his paper for some surface-structure errors, tells him to eliminate what she doesn't understand, and directs him to focus on what she does understand: "The field notes describing this interaction record the fact that following Mrs. Stone's instructions, 'Elliott gritted his teeth. Once back at his chair he slumped'" (46).

In her discussion of the two incidents, Michaels makes some very important points, not the least of which is that "the lack of shared cultural norms for telling a story, making a point, giving an explanation, and so forth can create barriers to understanding" (50). She also notes that, "In each case, the student was encouraged to leave out the text that the teacher found difficult to understand and difficult to connect to the initial topic" (50). The "good" news is that Elliott eventually produces an acceptable paragraph that "bore a striking resemblance to the rest of his classmates' pieces, in spite of the fact that they wrote about different circus acts" (48).

But the bad news overwhelms the good. Of course, at one level, given that the teacher edited Elliott's surface structure for him to retype, and given that she controlled the content and allowed him to keep only what she understood, it is reasonable to question whose essay it actually is! Instead of being encouraged and helped to learn how to revise his writing so that his ideas might be explored, developed, and articulated, Elliott is, essentially, forced to ignore and eliminate the content that matters to him and "shape" his paragraph into an acceptable *form*. Elliott is learning that what he cares about doesn't matter in school. And as a budding writer, he is learning that it is not *what* you think that matters but *how* you write/ say it. Instead of learning to use writing as part of a discovery process, as a heuristic, Elliott learns to avoid complex thinking. Instead of learning to use writing to express new and complex ideas, Elliott learns to use it to show that he can produce a correctly punctuated and shaped paragraph. In short, like so many students in our schools, Elliott is learning to *write writing*. And given the writing he is learning to write, one can hardly be surprised if Elliott decides that this is all a pretty silly exercise having little or nothing to do with his own existence.

These last comments, however, make it important for me to present my own qualifications here because some readers might choose to infer that I am so committed to the "process" of writing and learning to write that I have no concern for the product—what is written. And nothing could be further from the truth. This is particularly important because of the issues raised by Lisa Delpit in some articles I will be discussing momentarily. I am concerned *first* with content, and second, when the content deserves and needs polishing, I am concerned with style, usage, and punctuation. But always, substance first.

To polish an empty narrative is like polishing coal in hopes of producing a diamond. Real writers know that they must first discover the possible gems in the surrounding minerals and then begin the process of cutting, shaping, and polishing. Mining for precious metals and minerals takes time and work; it involves dead ends, cave-ins, frustrations, and disappointments. And sometimes, more often than most writers like to admit, the search produces little more than fool's gold or other worthless rocks. It is precisely because I am so very concerned with powerful writing that I stress *the processes* that most writers engage in as they try to write something of importance or value. Likewise, while I am concerned with helping students shape and polish their narratives once they have created narratives worthy of such work, I believe it is destructive to force them to do so in a singular, limited, and limiting form. And it is particularly ironic that students with the least experience in essayist literacy or edited American English are those who are often most pressured to produce polished pieces before any exploration takes place. Strong writers are often given considerable leeway in the schools. The less experienced writers, those who most need the opportunity to explore what it is they have to say and possible ways of saying/writing it are the ones most likely to be skilled and drilled to death.

As Michaels points out, teachers are often preoccupied with moving students toward facility in what is termed *essayist literacy*, the ability to write (and in Deena's case, speak) in a discourse that typifies the formal school essay: a clearly stated topic, a series of developed comments on and elaboration of that topic, and some sort of conclusion, often repeating what has been said. Writers often characterize this form as follows: "Tell 'em what you're going to say; say it; tell 'em what you said." (And while this developmental structure for writing can often be useful, we might ask ourselves how much "real" writing—writing that is not school related—is structured in this somewhat lifeless manner.) What is generally not accepted as good form in essayist literacy (in the United States, at least) are the kinds of variations introduced in Deena's oral discourse or Elliott's written discourse. One might add, however, that the highly developed discourse systems of fully literate Chinese, Japanese, Arabic, and other non-native speakers of English are also generally considered improper when evaluated in terms of the essayist literacy that is most typically honored and rewarded in American schools and colleges. In other words, we are not simply discussing a few students here (Collins, 1985).

As Michaels suggests, teachers' insistence on "simple, standardized texts often puts minority speakers [writers] of non-standard English at a disadvantage," even though the teachers may be motivated "by the best of intentions" (52). And it is at least reasonable to suggest that the intentions are sometimes based in misinformation and teacher bias. At the very least, it is imperative to note that the treatment of both Deena and Elliott grows out of the fact that neither teacher is primarily interested in the essential *content* of either student's utterances. In both cases, the students have made the mistake of trying to tell a story, narrate an event about which they genuinely care, not recognizing that the issue at hand is not *what* they have to say (write), but *how* they say (write) it that matters to those in power; the issue at hand is the organization, development, and usage they employ to say (write) their experience.

Again, it would be a mistake to respond by suggesting that this is all very sad for Deena and Elliott, but after all these are just two of many young students. If these were isolated examples, I suppose we might (somewhat insensitively) dismiss them. But the fact is that both Deena and Elliott grew up in primary Discourse systems that differ from those of their teachers and that differ from the Discourse system that is labeled as essayist or academic literacy. Many people grow up in highly oral Discourse systems, systems that delight in and expect associational webbing, call and response interactions. People of many cultures consciously avoid stating a thesis or main point so as not to insult the intelligence of the listener/reader. But for a variety of reasons, schools (and many other powerful societal institutions) often act as though essayist or academic literacy is the best and only acceptable way of telling a story or making a point or communicating in general. This would be an interesting enough fact if most people in the United States employed discourses that are reflected in essayist literacy, but if one were to consider the conversations going on all over this country in bars, at sports events, on playgrounds, at social gatherings of all kinds, on the farm, in the factories, even in college dormitories, I suspect even the casual observer would realize that essayist literacy, the Discourse system of the powers that be, is considerably less common than is often pretended. (Even *among* the powers that be? Now wouldn't that be interesting! A look back at Nixon's White House Tapes might be particularly revealing?) Consider, just for the fun of it (or the pain), the possibility that all this emphasis on essayist literacy and standard English has more to do with discriminating against minorities, with controlling people than it has to do with an honest (misguided) belief that essayist Discourse is somehow better than other kinds of Discourse systems? Consider the fact that the American "standard" is directly related, to the British standard, our colonizing forefathers. And, no matter how much Americans make fun of the snobbery of the British upper-crust and the "funny" way those Brits talk, isn't the joking usually accompanied by a grudging sense that "their way" is somehow more "proper" than ours? But leaving all that aside for the time being, let me move to the powerful voice of Lisa Delpit who has her own serious concerns about how non-dominant dialects and non-mainstream Discourse systems are treated in the schools (Delpit: 1986, 1988, 1992).

At first glance, Delpit appears to be arguing in favor of the kinds of teachers Michaels cites in her study. Delpit asserts that "some" teachers she refers to as "radical or progressive teachers of literacy" are "refusing to teach . . . the superficial features (e.g., grammar, form, style) of dominant Discourses." She goes on to say that these teachers "seek instead to develop literacy solely within the language and style of the students' home Discourse" (1992: 300). Clearly such a charge cannot be levied against the teachers Deena and Elliott experience.

Of course, given that the "some" Delpit refers to is a relatively vague group, it's difficult to argue with the initial point. I can only say that I have never met any of the group who comprise that "some." But one can hardly argue with Delpit's point that any teacher who "refuses" to teach students to participate in a broad range of discourses is irresponsible, to say the least. Again, it should be clear that the teachers in Michaels' study are failing to help their students participate in a broad range of discourses.

Delpit is essentially asserting that it is wrong to focus entirely on a student's primary Discourse, encouraging the use of an authentic voice in that discourse, to the complete exclusion of learning any other, secondary discourses. More specifically, she is arguing against those who would encourage African American students to speak and write in Black Vernacular and not teaching them the dominant Discourse of Standard English. And as long as we highlight the issue of "complete exclusion of learning any other, secondary discourses," I would fully agree with her. In fact, this is one of my own central points: exclusionary agendas in areas of language and discourse are dangerous and potentially victimizing.

When Delpit discusses what should be done, she echoes bell hooks: "The point must not be to eliminate students' home languages but rather to add other voices and Discourses to their repertoires. . . . [R]acism and oppression must be fought on as many fronts and in as many voices as we can muster" (1992: 301). In addition to trying to teach students to use secondary Discourses with facility, Delpit points out that teachers can "discuss openly the injustices of allowing certain people to succeed, based not upon merit but upon which family they were born into, which discourse they had access to as children. . . . We can again let our students know they can resist a system that seeks to limit them to the bottom rung of the social and economic ladder" (1992: 301). I would simply add this: to do less than this for and with our students is unethical and immoral.

While it is not necessary to argue against many of Delpit's major and important points, I do believe that certain qualifications are in order. I am particularly concerned with Delpit's suggestions that many teachers accept and encourage the Discourse systems that non-dominant speaker/writers bring into schools. First, I believe that one is more likely to find, in most schools, that the majority of teachers, whether they see themselves as liberatory pedagogists or not, stress standard English, their own somewhat distorted sense of the dominant discourse, and they do so through a focus on skills and drills that have little effect on the language production of the students in those classrooms. Second, as Delpit mentions, James Gee's work suggests that students are as unlikely to acquire the dominant Discourse in a classroom as they are to become fluent in a foreign language by studying its grammar, usage and vocabulary 40 minutes a day five days a week. You may be able to get there from here, but not through those kinds of doorways. Immersion in the new discourse(s), constant and repeated production of and experimentation with it orally and in writing—these may help the learner acquire the new ability.

Third, I believe that all students should have the right to choose among discourses, if they wish, and this clearly means that teachers have to help students become aware of the different discourses they may want to acquire. Likewise, it is essential that, in the process of helping students to see what choices are available and to find their own ways into those discourses, they continue to understand the importance and beauty of their own primary discourse. But having said this, I believe it is also absolutely essential that they understand that, while it may be beneficial to acquire dominant secondary discourses, in and of itself, this will not end the discrimination they are subject to because of their class, race, sex. . . . There are plenty of poor folk and people of color who speak and write perfectly good, standard English, but that hasn't necessarily altered their socioeconomic circumstances or the ways in which they are mistreated by a society that continues to discriminate against many groups and individuals. It is, after all, important to remember that while the media felt free to ignore the letters June Jordan's students had written in non-dominant dialect, the police and the press felt equally free to ignore Willie's letter which was written in the dominant dialect.

Teaching Li'l Abner: Geve me a brak!

Sometimes discussions of literacy and non-dominant English seem to focus almost exclusively on African Americans, Mexican Americans, Native Americans, and Puerto Ricans. Someone predisposed to racial and genetic stereotyping might choose to infer that differences in language and literacy, especially when those differences are perceived as deficits, are inherently associated with skin color and race. Of course, nothing could be further from the truth. This fact, however, does little to short circuit books like *The Bell Curve* and other repeated attempts to suggest that people of color (I wonder what people of no color look like?), particularly African Americans, are less intelligent and linguistically able than Anglos. The following discussion focusing on the language and (il)literacy of an Appalachian family, however, clearly indicates that language and Discourse systems are not color coded. In addition to further developing the discussion of the problems that non-dominant speakers meet in American schools and the failure of schools to help students acquire the dominant Discourse, it also shows that meanness and ignorance are color blind.

In her book, *Other People's Words*, Victoria Purcell-Gates, Director of the Literacy Laboratory at the Harvard Graduate

School of Education, relates her two-year experience of tutoring an Appalachian woman named Jenny and her son Donny, neither of whom can read. The family, also including Big Donny, the father, and Timmy, a four-year-old sibling are "urban Appalachians," a group below African Americans on the educational ladder with a 40–75% dropout rate (33). Jenny and her family are illiterate, unable to read food labels, street signs, print of any kind. Jenny has found herself up against a wall of indifference and ignorance in trying to get help for her son Donny through his school. But Jenny is doggedly devoted to her son, and she sincerely wants to learn to read both for herself and so that she can help her son, Donny, with his school work. Donny can write only his name and read the word *the* with assistance but he has been passed on into second grade regardless of these facts. Of course, he cannot do his homework because he cannot read, and his teacher's response to the lack of homework is to penalize him by giving him more written homework. If Joseph Heller had not already written *Catch-22*, this situation would certainly provide a model for that infamous "catch."

The family lives in a virtually print-free home: there is a family Bible, but no one ever opens it because they can't read; they incidentally ended up with some books printed in German, but they don't even know it is a foreign language because all print is a foreign language. These facts, however, do not indicate stupidity or complete separation from the outer world: they enjoy television and Big Donny is an avid viewer of videotapes on natural history and historical events. Far from being a disinterested parent, Jenny has gone to school officials countless times complaining about the situation, but they pay no attention to her whatsoever until the professional, Purcell-Gates demands their attention. That the treatment Jenny has received is directly related, at least in part, to her dialect is emphasized when one of Donny's teachers who has met Jenny tells Purcell-Gates: "I *knew* she was ignorant as soon as she opened her mouth!" (37).

In her attempt to find out why Jenny never learned to read, Purcell-Gates asks Jenny about her own school experiences. Having moved to the city when she was three, settling in an "urban Appalachian 'ghetto'" Jenny went to public schools (18–

19). Jenny believes that she could not learn to read because of the way she speaks, a victim of both the implementation of an uncompromising phonics approach and classroom ridicule for the way she talks: her stigmatized dialect and "inability" to pronounce words "correctly" lead to ridicule and her belief that she is unable to learn how to read (Purcell-Gates: 26, 164; see also, Blanton in Dillard). And the desire and energy she brings to ending this cycle of illiteracy both for herself and her children is more than a little impressive, especially given the fact that the very institution that should be helping her— the school—dismisses her and her son entirely.

Of course, the school's treatment of her son has already taken a tremendous toll. Donny has little interest in or understanding of what school is about, partly because he cannot read and partly because the teachers have pretty much decided that he is doomed to failure anyway and therefore pay him no attention. For example, in response to one drill calling for Donny to "write words that fit in the blanks" of a set of sentences, Donny "measured each word with his two index fingers, moved them to the blanks and matched word to sentence according to the perceived 'fit'" (Purcell-Gates: 63). Of course, none of the sentences made any sense to him, so this was both a reasonable and somewhat ingenious strategy. As Purcell-Gates points out, the school had helped Donny learn "about letters and forms as these applied to the writing of his name and to the recognition and printing of the letters of the alphabet. He had, however, almost no implicit notions of the vocabulary, syntax, or decontextualized nature of written language as found in books, letters, environmental signs, written directions, or personal notices" (63). In short, print means nothing to Donny; he has "no sense that print operates as a code" (64).

The world of skills and drills has had almost no impact on Donny whatsoever, and it has similarly victimized Jenny. In an attempt to find out what exactly Jenny can or cannot read, Purcell-Gates has her "read" out of workbooks she has been using in a community reading program for adults staffed by volunteers. As Jenny "read" from the workbook exercises, Purcell-Gates gets "the clear impression that she viewed the task of reading as one of remembering isolated words, one at a time, with no sense of language structure or meaning": as

Jenny says of her own reading of the words, "I can read 'em in here [the workbook], but if they're anywheres else, I don't know 'em."

And yet, even given these conditions, Jenny and Donny do progress. In a very real sense, the progress that both Donny and Jenny make is agonizingly slow and amazingly fast: it is slow because at the end of two years, Donny has made minimal progress, but given the fact that he has to make up for 11 years of non-literacy, of having almost no contact with print whatsoever and having no idea that it is a code or potentially meaningful, his progress is fast. Purcell-Gates focused instruction on phonics for about one-quarter of each lesson, but the rest of the time is used for activities that are often associated with a whole language approach. Donny "composes" orally, and the teacher types up the composition to help him see that print is related to what he has said. She often reads to him; she tries to get him to write for himself. She uses a full range of language activities. He eventually manages to do some writing using invented spellings (IMI=I am I). And given that he started from nowhere, his progress holds some promise.

But the simple fact is that Donny is a passive-aggressive resistor when it comes to print literacy, and this may be one of Purcell-Gates's most disturbing and significant findings. Clearly school held little promise for Donny: why should he care about an institution or its values when those who run it seem to care so little about him? In addition, no one whom Donny might wish to emulate was print literate, so he clearly lacked literacy models. But perhaps the most significant factor in Donny's resistance, second only to the school's failure to recognize him as a potential learner, was firmly planted in the fact that, "as a male child, his identity was increasingly tied to his father, who had repeatedly announced his lack of desire to learn to read" (150). Big Donny "hunted, fished, and drove four-wheelers"; he was a "'doer' and a 'maker' not a reader or a writer." And so also would Donny perceive himself: the adult male culture was proving to be far stronger than one teacher's influence. And yet it also seems clear that Donny's emulation of his immediate adult male culture is particularly powerful because the culture of the school offered him no entry: quite the opposite; it offered him ridicule and failure. From my own perspective, especially if I try to think from the perspective of an 11-year-old, Big Donny looks like a good choice.

Jenny, on the other hand, is not 11 years old and does not approve of all of Big Donny's ways; she desperately wants to learn to read and write. And she makes exceptional progress. At the end of two years she is composing her own journal entries, writing letters (her spellings often reflect the phonological features of her dialect: "pike" for "pick," "pecher" for "picture," "geve" for "give") (121–130).

Purcell-Gates presents us with a powerful description of the plight of this specific family along with all the suggestiveness it holds for us as we think of other non-literate groups. But while the story of Jenny, and to some extent Donny holds promise, it should also, it seems to me, cause us to take seriously Purcell-Gates's description of the exclusion these people and others like them experience: "Donny and Jenny as learners, each in his or her own time, and Jenny as a mother stood outside of a solid wall of indifference and cultural elitism and ignorance" (157).

One can imagine Aretha Franklin asking what it will take to get some *R-E-S-P-E-C-T* for Deena and Elliott and Jenny and Donny an all the people like them who be dissed and beat by those in power who treat them like trash cause the way they talk. What will it tak to geve Jenny and Donny the brak they deserve? And why people like teachers and such don't be helping? Maybe it the way they talk, you dig?

Raymond

Is not his real name. But he is real people. Some years ago, one of the writing tutors I work with at the College Learning Center came to me to ask for advice about how to help a student. The tutor told me that Raymond was failing freshmen composition, that his written work was highly non-standard, and she was afraid that, even with her help, he would still fail. I quickly inferred that the tutor felt that Raymond was being mistreated by the teacher, and she was absolutely correct. I got Raymond to come and see me, asking him to bring some of his written work. A Nuyorican who had moved to the city when he was 14, Raymond spoke distinctly non-dominant, but perfectly intelligible English, highly influenced by Black Vernacular. The first essay of his he showed me was covered with coded marks referring him to a grammar-usage handbook to correct the many "mistakes" he had made in the paper—almost all of them directly related to his oral dialect. At the top of the page, the teacher had written, "*E*—this is not acceptable in college. You need help." Raymond leaned over my desk as I looked at the paper, pointed to the note at the top, and said angrily, "Raymond know he need help; he just don't know how to get it!" Knowing full well that a confrontation with this colleague would do nothing to help Raymond, I had him change in to my section of the course and he began writing personal narratives. Slowly, very slowly, with my help and the help of that very sensitive tutor, Raymond began to learn how to produce relatively standard English. Because of his work in my class and with the tutor, he became a major fan of peer-editing, realizing that it was only with such feedback and multiple revisions that his written work would be acceptable to his other professors. Toward the end of this particular semester, Raymond turned in a paper that clearly had not been written by him: not only was it in perfectly standard English, but it even contained correctly punctuated compound-complex sentences and was about a classical music concert. When I asked him if he had written the paper, he smiled and immediately confirmed that he had not. A friend had written it for him. Like many of us, of course, I take plagiarism seriously, but I had seldom met a plagiarist so quick to admit to the act. When I asked him why he had done this, he said, "Oh, Dr. Courts, you have worked so hard with me all semester, I think you deserve at least one good paper from me!"

We discussed plagiarism and he promised he would never do this again; he clearly had never intended any serious deception. He just wanted to reward me. Three and one-half years passed before I saw him again. He stood just inside my office door and said, "You probably don't remember me, yes?" He was maturer looking, but the smile was still the same. And he was pleased that I remembered him. He told me that he was about to graduate with a degree in sociology and was then on his way to graduate school with an academic scholarship. He also said that his writing was the thing that had gotten him such good grades and that he never turned in a paper without first getting peer-editing and doing multiple revisions.

I'm still not exactly sure how I feel about the entire episode, but I know that when I read Villanueva's comments about "racelessness," about learning standard English as a process of erasing his heritage, I immediately thought of Raymond. On the other hand, I forced nothing on Raymond. He made his own choices, and he made them work. More than anything, I hope that, instead of erasing the voice he had when I first met him, he gained some new voices that gave him entry to the world of academia. One point, however, is glaringly clear to me. No good whatsoever would have been done to fail Raymond in freshmen composition. Both he and I knew, explicitly, that the *C+* I had given him was a recognition of the hard work he had done. And he fully understood that he needed to make considerably more progress if his written work was to serve him well in college. It was a simple fact that most of my work with Raymond focused on helping him organize and develop his ideas. My hope was that as he gained control over the content he was writing about, his increased work in writing and the feedback he could get from a writing tutor would eventually help him standardize his grammar, usage, and punctuation. Apparently, he made it work.

Gender Issues: You've come a long way baby (so couldn't you just quiet down now?)

While reading literature across a broad varieties of cultures and countries as I prepared a graduate course in the teaching of multicultural literatures, one central, upsetting fact evidenced itself over and over: women are universally discriminated against and mistreated. Bought, sold, and enslaved in some countries; murdered indiscrimately in others; unable to get a hearing on harassment charges in the United States Senate: John Lennon was right. Commenting on the status of feminism in our own educational institutions, Lynda Stone suggests that feminism is ignored and its adherents marginalized in educational institutions because of a prevailing point of view that we no longer need feminism because most of the "problems for women in education" have been solved or are being solved (148). Obviously, critical pedagogy must directly and regularly interrogate, uncover, and try to eliminate such a widespread debasement of human beings.

But what if anything does this have to do with Discourse systems? The question does not, as nearly as I can tell, give way to widely accepted generalizations.

The work of Robin Lakoff, for example, suggests that women's speech is characterized by hesitations, declaratives marked by rising intonations suggesting tentativeness, and various aspects that qualify and undermine the force of a given utterance (Lakoff, 1975). She also raises the issue of whether women should try to acquire characteristics of male discourse or maintain their more open and communal style of discourse (Lakoff, 1990). Relying on the unpublished work of Evelyn Ashton-Jones, Irene Ward suggests that in the mixed-sex situations she studies, women were "more likely to assume responsibility for maintaining the dialogue and, yet, have fewer opportunities to initiate conversations that are sustained by their male counterparts. Men interrupted or overlapped in conversational situations from seventy-five to ninety-six percent of the time when the conversation was among mixed-sex conversants" (85–86).

But both Ward and Jennifer Coates also problematize the discussion by raising class/race issues. Ward first discusses various writers who characterize women's Discourse as essentially collaborative, sensitive, non-assertive, and associative—open and exploratory; but second, she points out that much of the work that has been done in this area has focused on white, middle-class, educated women and has not often included the Discourse of minority women and women from lower classes. Maureen Hourigan echoes this concern when she writes "that the open-ended, exploratory, and often autobiographical writing associated with feminist pedagogy is not appropriate for groups marginalized by other factors in their relation to language. . . . [A]utobiographical writing may even silence women marginalized by both class and gender" (Hourigan: xvii).

Ward extends this kind of concern, pointing to the problem created by feminism's "almost wholesale adoption of collaborative learning." She believes that collaborative learning can misfire at times because of the ways in which gender and class roles are played out in both small and large discussion groups. Again relying on the work of Evelyn Ashton-Jones, Ward points out that marginalized groups (women, certain ethnic groups, students from "lower" socioeconomic groups) do not have equal status in collaborative learning situations and are often either silenced or pressured into conformity (84): "Unfortunately, the uneven power relationships that affect the social context of composition classrooms often are 'invisible' because they reproduce in our actions and speech the socially inscribed and largely unexamined assumptions and stereotypes that comprise social relations in society at large, even though educators often desire, with the best intentions, to view their classrooms as 'neutral spaces' or 'level playing fields' where all students receive an equal chance to learn" (85). And gender is clearly one of the "'invisible' ways."

I find myself more than a little ill at ease about making any generalizations about gender and Discourse. Fortunately, I don't think that this causes an immediate problem at the classroom level because the approaches I suggest in Chapter 5 do not rely on absolute definitions of anyone's Discourse system as much as they ask teachers to help students become conscious of their own Discourse systems and those of others so that they can begin to make choices for themselves about how they wish to speak and write under any set of circumstances.

My own experiences with female students at both the high school and college levels suggests that women are often silenced in classrooms, and the silence results from a variety of factors. Younger female students often appear unwilling to challenge the males in the class, perhaps because Lakoff is correct in characterizing them as having been brought up in a submissive Discourse system. On the other hand, the silence of the females also reminds me of the silence that I sometimes see among minority students in classrooms where the student population is predominantly white. I generally do not read this silence to be a sign of submissiveness as much as a sign of distrust of the dominant power structure. In conferencing with female students and minority students about this silence, individuals from both groups have told me (when they decide to confide in me) that they were simply not going to expose their real thoughts and feelings to a group that might use such honesty against them. Although I am paraphrasing, both sets of individuals say something like this: The sexists (racists) in the class will remain silent or treat me with contempt and the others don't need to hear what they already know.

But again, while I would not pretend to have solved such a complex problem, I have found that writing and role-playing activities that enable writers to say what they think and feel *through some other point of view that allows them some personal distance*—a character they've created, for example—allow these important issues to come to the fore and at least threaten the silence that too often occurs.

My own feeling is that as long we provide ample opportunity for women, and everyone else, to use and explore their own primary Discourse systems as well as those of other groups, creating situations that short circuit the possibility of other, more dominant Discourses to silence them, we will improve on the present situation considerably. Finally, I strongly agree with Lynda Stone who argues the need for a "common memory": "A common memory for feminists looks something like this: continued attention to opposing sexist oppression and upholding sisterhood, continued legitimation of the personal and self-conscious, continued valuing of critique out of diversity, continued development of an evolving theoretical base, continued recognition of central 'historical' concern—issues of body and voice, of public life and equality, of processes of collective understanding and action" (150).

Whose Right: Who's Right?

Some people, including me, think that everyone has a right to his/her own language—even students. Not just a right to use it at home or on the playground or on the farm or in the hills of West Virginia, but even in the hallowed halls and classrooms of the dominant institutions. We believe that no one should have to suffer for exercising that right. And this issue of one's right to one's own language allows me to present one more powerful voice in the discussion—the voice of Geneva Smitherman, who quotes from a statement passed by the Executive Committee of the Conference of College Composition and Communication: "We affirm the students' right to their own patterns and varieties of language—the dialects of their nurture or whatever dialects in which they find their own identity and style. Language scholars long ago denied that the myth of a standard American dialect has any validity. The claim that any dialect is unacceptable amounts to an attempt of one social group to exert its dominance over another. Such a claim leads to false advice for speakers and writers, and immoral advice for humans. A nation proud of its diverse heritage and its cultural and racial variety will preserve its heritage of dialects. We affirm strongly that teachers must have the experiences and training that will enable them to respect diversity and uphold the right of students to their own language" (Smitherman, 1995: 21).

But "rights" are funny things. A friend once said to me, "I have the right to walk through that park at night and no one has the right to stop me or bother me." She said this in a state of rage after having been mugged in Central Park. Though I kept my mouth shut in the moment, it occurred to me that having that right did nothing whatsoever to stop her from being victimized. As I've thought about this over the years, I still puzzle over the right response to her statement because her victimization and consequent assertion that she had rights that should prevent any such victimization seem particularly relevant to what goes on in schools and society regarding foreign students and students who speak/write dialects that are considered non-standard.

Just as this woman surely has the right to walk through Central Park at night, so also students (should) have the right to their own language. One initial difference, however, in the analogy is that, although the woman does, by law, have the right to walk through Central park at night, even though that right may be trampled by criminals, our students' right to their own language is not guaranteed by law, and nothing an intelligent, sensitive group of English teachers say at a Conference necessarily changes that fact. Indeed, one is much more likely to hear legislators arguing for "English Only" legislation than one is likely to hear them arguing for legal protection for students' right to their own language.

But I happen to agree strongly with the students' right to their own language, so for the time being, let me continue to examine the analogical relationships between the woman's experience and the experience of our students. She exercised her right and was mugged and beaten. It made her angry and fearful; it forced her to think once again about the absolute vulnerability that so many women in our society feel as they walk down streets or through the corridors of corporate power; it made me think of the sexual harassment allegations made by Anita Hill against Clarence Thomas. Having rights doesn't necessarily stop any one from being mugged or harassed or mistreated, but sometimes it allows the person who has been victimized to seek justice against the abusers. On the other hand, much of the time, in many modern societies including our own, victims find that the justice system does little to eliminate or change the fact of their victimization. My friend's rights have little to do with the fact that she does not walk through Central Park at night and she tries to avoid walking there at all. In fact, she tries to avoid walking alone at night at any time. So much for that "right."

But back to the rights of our students for the moment. Even if the profession agreed that students have a right to their own language (and I will examine that "if" momentarily), and even if legislators legally guaranteed such a right, they would still find themselves, like my friend, solitary and beaten in the metaphorical Central Park of the Dominant Discourse of Essayist Literacy or Edited American English or "good" English or "Standard" English. In this case, the muggers would prevent them from getting certain jobs, deny them access to college educations, demoralize them so much that they would leave high school before graduating—in short, they would learn the fear and anger and impotence of my friend; they would stay off the streets that are owned and run by those who control language and education. A few, of course, learn to navigate, to be more careful about where they walk (and how they speak); some might learn to carry the weapon of essayist literacy and turn it against the power structure, but most of them would know that it is more than their language that bothers the powers that be—there's all those different colors of their skins. . . . There are all those things like class, and race, and sex that get in the way. Still, the weapon helps a little; keeps the victimizers a little off guard.

But as I said earlier, not everyone, in fact not many people in power, agree fully or even in part with the statement passed by the membership of CCCC. Even the National Council of

Teachers of English (to which CCCC is institutionally related) found the language of CCCC a little too strong: "First, the NCTE resolution distinguishes between spoken and written language in relationship to student's dialects, and although it 'accept(s) the linguistic premise that all these dialects are equally efficient as systems of communication,' the resolution goes on to 'affirm' that students should learn the 'conventions of what has been called written edited American English'" (NCTE Resolution #74.2, 1974. Quoted in Smitherman, 1995: 23).

In other words, CCCC believed that, "one may choose roles which imply certain dialects, but the decision is a social one, for the dialect itself does not limit the information which can be carried, and the attitudes may be most clearly conveyed in the dialect the writers finds most congenial. . . ." (CCCC, 1974: 8. Quoted in Smitherman, 1995: 23).

But the best that NCTE could agree to was that English teachers should "promote classroom practices to expose students to the variety of dialects that occur in our multi-regional, multi-ethnic, and multi-cultural society, so that they too will understand the nature of American English and come to respect all its dialects (NCTE Resolution #74.2, 1974. Quoted in Smitherman, 1995: 23). By the way, although I did and do agree with CCCC's position articulated earlier, I intend no cheap shots here at NCTE. This was 1974 and both groups were wrestling with serious and complex issues, and as Smitherman points out, both groups produced documents and resolutions that represent "a compromise . . . born of the contradictions among radicals, moderates, and conservatives" (1995: 24). That NCTE was more conservative than CCCC doesn't change the fact that, even in 1995, both positions remain essentially rejected by the *practices* that characterize most American schools from kindergarten through graduate school. Even with all the talk and scholarship about multiculturalism and "difference," one finds scholars in these areas absolutely committed to Edited American English or Essayist Literacy. It sometimes seems as though the profession can entertain all kinds of differences in human beings—the single and powerful exception being Discourse systems. As Smitherman so powerfully states: "In spite of recently reported gains in black student writing, chronicled by the NAEP and higher scores on the SAT, the rate of functional illiteracy and drop-outs among America's underclass [*not limited to African Americans*] is moving faster than a Concorde. A genuine recognition of such students' culture and language is desperately needed if we as a profession are to play some part in stemming this national trend. I write genuine because, in spite of the controversy surrounding policies like the 'Students' right to Their Own Language,' the bicultural, bilingual model has *never* really been tried. Lip service is about all most teachers gave it. . . ." (1995: 25).

Indeed, anyone conversant with educational language policies knows, whether we focus on bi-dialectal, bilingual, or multilingual education, and particularly as policies are implemented in classrooms, educational practice focuses primarily on language *shift* rather than language *maintenance*: "That is, the philosophy of using the native language as a vehicle to teach and eventually *shift* native speakers *away from their home language*, vs. a social and pedagogical model that teaches the target language—in this country English—while providing support for *maintaining the home language*—Spanish, Polish, Black English, etc. All along, despite a policy like the 'Students' Right,' the system has just been perping—engaging in fraudulent action" (1995: 25).

Given this last paragraph, one might argue that the real fraud is in asserting that we really can achieve both, that acquisition of new Discourse systems will not significantly modify old ones, but such an accusation cuts across some fine lines that deserve careful distinction. Clearly, some people are multilingual and bi-dialectal, and while they may, as Gee asserts, be identified as not being fully fluent in a given language or dialect, they are still at something of an advantage over those of us who do not have such linguistic mobility. Even qualifying Smitherman's position from this point of view, it does not change the fact that *bi-* dialectalism/lingualism—fluency in several Discourse systems—does not often appear to be the agenda of schools. To the extent that learners are helped to understand that as they language *within* new Discourse systems their primary Discourse system will probably undergo change, they are not being victimized.

But Smitherman's reflections on past CCCC and NCTE resolutions about students' rights to their own language goes well beyond a recounting of old positions. She suggests that we are at the beginning of a paradigm shift "from a provincial, more narrowly conceived focus to a broader internationalist perspective," and presents statements from the CCCC 1988 "National Language Policy" resolution to itemize the new agenda: "1. To provide resources to enable native and non-native speakers to achieve oral and literate competence in English, the language of wider communication; 2. To support programs that assert the legitimacy of native languages and dialects and ensure that proficiency in the mother tongue will not be lost; and 3. To foster the teaching of languages other than English so that native speakers of English can rediscover the language of their heritage or learn a second language" (1995: 26).

In the face of shrinking budgets throughout the nation's schools and colleges, increasing conservatism in many governmental and educational agencies, movements like English Only and the politics of far right Catholicism, Protestantism, and Islamic fundamentalism, and ethnocentrically based monoculturalism as represented by presidential candidates like Pat Buchanan, and religious leaders like Pat Robertson or Farakhan, it would be easy to dismiss Smitherman's and CCCC's directives as doomed to failure. But those of us in education need to remember that systems don't change by themselves; people change them. Instead of hiding from the various theoretical positions and demagoguery associated with them, we need to have students actively engage the language and content of the Buchanans, et al. If we genuinely do not want them to be unconsciously constructed by the messages that surround them, we must engage them in a critical examination of the media(ted) and linguistic world in which they are immersed.

As Aronowitz and Giroux point out, "What is at stake here is the development of a border pedagogy that can fruitfully work to break down those ideologies, cultural codes, and social practices that prevent students from recognizing how social forms at particular historical conjunctures operate to repress alternative readings of their own experiences, society, and the world" (1991: 121). But any attempt to move from the concept of a border pedagogy toward praxis demands a theoretical base on which to found classroom methodologies, a theory of language and learning that allows and encourages students to actively engage in an examination of their own worlds *as those worlds interface with the larger world around them.* Those people who have been marginalized must be given the opportunity to move to the center of the page; others have to be given the opportunity to see that a page exists, a page on which they might wish to begin using their own voices to create and inscribe their selves.

A Voice from the Margin

The following essay was written by a first semester college student for one of the first assignments in a required freshmen composition course. I do not know the student. The teacher guaranteed him anonymity if his paper was used publicly in any way. The paper had been distributed in class for peer-editing and discussion, as had all the others students' papers. The teacher brought it to me asking for ideas about how to help the writer. I use it here for several reasons: (1) it clearly evidences non-dominant dialect; (2) as best I can tell the writer writes authentically and with commitment; and (3) it evidences characteristics common to oral narrative. The assignment was fairly typical, and the teacher simply wanted to get the students writing so s/he could get a sense of their writing abilities. Students were to find an article in the campus newspaper (the *Leader*) that interested them, briefly summarize the article and follow the summary with an opinion or commentary on the article. Here is one result, typed exactly as I received it, except for the one bracketed proper name.

Date Rape on Campus

This week in the leader, they had a issue the fill the front page about a female who was sexual abuse in front of lacogsse [LoGrasso] hall the man was caught. But the things that got me is that It was his second offense. Today this issue is growing like crazy what make it hard to prevent that It mostly people they know.

So people that date rape doesn't really exist, that the female starts the whole things. That what the female wears, makes the male or person feel thay can take control of the female.

In my opinion I feel that there should be more protest of the campus. More policemans on the campus will help cut down on the terror that makes the women undefense. The female them selfs must learn to choose there mates a lot more carefully. If the campus It self can make or design course, so they can focus on the problem.

Date rape is the most leading talked about issue on the campus today. This incident in fredonia, is just one of the thousands situation that happened today on the campus and college life. So with the help of people and banning together, one day we can all findly put a end to this terror crime, called "sexually harassed".

Clearly my analysis of this paper is shaped by everything I've been discussing in this and the last chapter. Readers can judge for themselves whether or not it appears valid. My own rule of thumb when reading student papers is to read them in good faith, trying, as Peter Elbow suggests, to "like" their work. Elbow suggests the following: "Underneath it all—suffusing the whole evaluative enterprise—let's learn to be better likers: liking our own and our students' writing, and realizing that liking need not get in the way of clear-eyed evaluation" (Elbow, 1992: 205). And the more I have read and thought about his paper, the more I like it. Note, I am *not* suggesting that it is acceptable or well written as it stands. I suspect that many readers would immediately suggest that paper's major problem lies in its use of non-dominant dialect, misspellings, omitted words, incomplete sentences, and run-ons. But I believe that this student has something important to say and that, at present, the major problem is one of underdevelopment of significant points, an underdevelopment that would be no problem whatsoever if the student was saying this to someone as part of a give and take (call and response) dialogue. Moreover, I would argue that many of the surface structure "errors" are errors only to the extent that they are not normally acceptable in *written*, academic prose: i.e., in almost every sense, this is a very *oral* piece of writing.

Let's take a closer look. Like some of the Discourse systems discussed above, the central point of the essay is not clearly stated at the beginning: it emerges. The writer begins by trying to fulfill the assignment: This article was in the newspaper, and it was about a man who touched the buttocks of two females in front of a campus building. Of course, the writer does not summarize at all, perhaps reasoning that a summary of something that everyone already read is unnecessary, or perhaps he simply doesn't know how to summarize. But by the second sentence of the opening paragraph, it is clear that the writer has already begun a transition to a topic that he *really* is incensed about—not only sexual harassment, but date rape.

The second paragraph moves directly to the topic of date rape, but fails to offer the necessary detail and exemplification that one normally expects in fully developed text-based prose. Again, however, I have the sense of the writer acting as though he is in a conversation in which the other participants already know and agree with much of what is being said. It almost feels as though it is set up with a call-response setting in mind. As a reader, try this: at the end of each paragraph say to yourself, "Word up!" or, "Yeah, Tell it like is!" This may help you get a sense of what I'm getting at here.

Paragraph three is fascinating because it does exactly what good arguments are supposed to do. The writer makes suggestions for dealing with the problem, and he also indicates that his is a sophisticated understanding of the problem, noting that everyone must be more careful, women included, to avoid such attacks.

The final paragraph is the least oral of the four and sounds more like "school writing" than anything else in the essay. And yet, at the same time, the writer repeats one of the key words in the essay—*terror*—to hammer home once more what he sees to be the central impact of date rape. Without ever saying so (writing it), the writer appears to be saying that sexual harassment of all kinds, date rape in particular, is really about the kinds of abuse and terror to which females in our society are regularly submitted.

Given that I do not know the writer at all, this may sound silly, but I *hear* this writer's voice. I hear him being sincerely upset about something that matters to him, and I hear him moving between his own oral voice and an attempt to use more formal "academic" language (albeit mistakenly). But that is exactly the point: this is someone who is in the constructive "mistake making" stage, trying to acquire a Discourse he has almost no experience with whatsoever. To begin by focusing this writer on the "errors" is, I believe, to guarantee that he will learn very little. First we must learn to work with what the writer writes—not with what is lacking but with what is potentially powerful. In conferencing with this writer, the teacher can ask him to talk more (and then write) about examples for the second paragraph. He can be asked to provide more details about implementing the suggested solutions in the third paragraph. Indirectly, at first, and later directly, he needs to learn that in text based prose, the writer must provide more information *because* there is no immediate possibility for call and response dialogue.

Next, I think the writer can be told directly that the name of the hall was spelled correctly in the newspaper and he needs to be more careful about reproducing correct spellings. In terms of the omitted words, he may simply need to read his paper aloud to discover them for himself. Or he may need a listener to help him become aware of them. I would, however, be surprised if he had reread the paper at all before handing it in, perhaps because he never had to before. I say this because I am fairly sure that this person has had little previous writing experience of any kind. Work on syntax and dialect, in any formal sense would come last, but if the conferencing had been successful, if the teacher had been tape recording or keeping a written record of what the writer said when asked to develop or restate certain points, I suspect that issues of syntax and dialect might be broached as part of that process.

My own central points here are these. Looked at positively, this paper has tremendous potential. As a reader, I need only convince the writer that *because I care* as much as he does about the issue, I want him to provide more information and learn to develop his ideas more fully and clearly. Otherwise his essay represents little more than another partially articulated outcry. Equally important, he needs to develop and articulate his ideas so that *he* better understands the complexity of the issue, especially insofar as he believes that the "female them selfs must learn to choose there mates a lot more carefully." Both he and I need to know if he is "blaming the victim" here. Likewise, he needs to care enough to polish the essay after he has more fully developed it, and I will be happy to help him do that. During that process, we can begin to talk about dialect and Discourse differences.

In the next chapter, I offer a theoretical/philosophical approach to the teaching of language and literacy that is based on some of the best information we have about how human beings learn. Equally important, it is a theoretical position that allows for the productive inclusion of various Discourse communities as well as allowing for the possibility of a critical pedagogy that is neither oppressive nor self-righteous—a pedagogy that is genuinely liberatory. At the same time, the following chapter presents a theory of multiple intelligences that destroys one of the most time-honored myths that schools and society have used for categorizing, pigeonholing, and "tracking" learners: *I*ntelligence *Q*uotients.

Chapter 4

Whole Language and Multiple Intelligences: Who You Think You Foolin'?

Theory . . . is the sort of talk we talk when a consensus breaks down, when we begin to disagree about fundamental principles and to argue about which principles are truly fundamental. . . . [I]n a state of theory people ask us to define or clarify our terms, and start contesting those definitions and categories. (Richter: 8)

We must look . . . at meaningful performances within a culture. Whereas intelligence tests look only at the individual, intelligence [tests] must take into account both individuals and societies. Even when intelligence tests have attempted to measure what we are calling individual competences, they have been narrow in scope. Rather than examining the range of human cognition, they have focused on a thin band of human cognitive competences . . . on certain aspects of linguistic and logical intelligence. Intelligence tests are limited not only in the competences that they examine, but in the way they examine them. (Gardner, 1993: 242)

I want to begin by making my own biases clear: First, I support the whole language approach to teaching, at all educational levels, because I believe it is supported by the best information we presently have about how human beings learn. In terms of the prior discussion of primary and secondary Discourses, a whole language approach to teaching offers a direct and focused set of principles that can be used by teachers to help students in several ways: (1) students can use and polish their primary Discourses at the same time they *learn* more about the nature of those Discourses and have an opportunity to take some pride in their primary Discourses instead of having them attacked or ignored in school; (2) they can *learn* about secondary Discourses—differences among them, uses/misuses of them, and ways in which they impact on the students' primary Discourses; and (3) they can engage in the process of *acquiring* secondary Discourses which they find to be useful or appropriate for their own needs.

Unfortunately, though not surprisingly, the whole language approach meets with considerable hostility from some people in the educational establishment who fear its emphasis on the students' experiences and articulations of those experiences. I see many of the attacks on the whole language movement to be firmly rooted in a desire to maintain what Paulo Freire refers to as the "banking" model of education, a model characterized by all-powerful teachers delivering knowledge to students whose job it is to memorize the knowledge (1971: 67). I also believe, however, that the whole language movement is sometimes surrounded by confusion because it is too often defined primarily through the idiosyncratic classroom practices of individual teachers rather than through the learning theories that form the foundation of the whole language approach. Indeed it is only through a valid and constructive theory of learning that teachers can generate classroom practices designed to meet the individual needs of different students as students evidence such needs.

If the whole language approach is viewed as a single method or frozen set of methods, it risks being viewed and attacked as little more than another educational fad. As an *approach* to teaching *founded in theory*, however, the whole language approach offers a basis for generating tremendous change in schools and schooling, particularly because it recognizes and embraces *difference* in students' abilities and intelligences.

I ask the reader to try to keep the following distinctions clearly in mind throughout the discussion of whole language: classroom *practices* grow out of a whole language *approach* to teaching; the whole language approach to teaching is supported by cognitive learning *theory*. I stress the distinctions because when such distinctions are lost, I believe confusion about the "whole language approach" enters at a gallop.

The second bias I will discuss in this chapter is related to theories of intelligence and the "measuring" of intelligence (IQ scores). By now, many readers are aware of the controversy surrounding the publication of *The Bell Curve* (Hernstein and Murray). Much of the publicity surrounding the book was based on its assertion of intelligence as an ethnically/racially controlled factor:

The difference in test scores between African-Americans and European-Americans as measured in dozens of reputable studies has converged on approximately a one standard deviation difference for several decades. Translated into centiles, this means that the average white person tests higher than about 84 percent of the population of blacks and that the average black person tests higher than about 16 percent of the population of whites.

The average black and white differ in IQ at every level of socioeconomic status (SES), but they differ more at high levels of SES than at low levels. Attempts to explain the difference in terms of test bias have failed. (269)

This is clearly a powerful statement, though the racial spin it presents is not terribly new—for that matter, almost nothing in this *Curve* is new. But the claim in the above quote is dangerous and misleading: *dangerous* because it presents an indefensible racial argument—black folks just aren't as smart as white folks (though "East Asians" score higher than whites on IQ tests and therefore are, presumably, smarter [269]); *misleading* because, as has been the case for decades, all of the arguments in the book are based on what is arguably a fiction. The fiction? First that there is such a thing as *g* (a single general factor of intelligence); second that *g* (IQ) is measured "most accurately" by IQ tests; and third, that IQ tests are not "biased against social, economic, ethnic, or racial groups" (22–23). Furthermore, the research base used by Hernstein and Murray, aside from being dated, is seriously tainted by their heavy reliance on the writings of "scholars linked to *Mankind Quarterly* . . . a notorious journal of 'racial history' founded, and funded, by men who believe in the genetic superiority of the white race" (Lane: 14).

Given the kinds of sources used in *The Bell Curve*, and the sometimes inaccurate/deceptive spin the authors use in reporting some of the research they cite (Lane: 14–19), one is inclined to substitute the word *spit-ball* for *curve* (Steinberg, 1996). And I should hardly be surprised by the quick and easy dismissal the book gives to Howard Gardner's work on multiple intelligences. Given Howard Gardner's theory of multiple intelligences, most fully explained in his 1983 publication *Frames of Mind*, and given the *Curve's* essential ignoring of that theory, I can only assume that a book as flawed as *The Bell Curve* was published primarily for its appeal to racist notions about human intelligence. But Gardner's work on multiple intelligences is important, not only because it rejects the relatively useless, reductivist systems that have been used for measuring IQ over the past decades, but because his theory recognizes the tremendous range of complexities involved in trying to describe human cognition and performance potential through the use of a single score based on someone's test: instead of participating in the circular, past practice of defining intelligence in terms of the test used to measure it, Gardner begins by daring to ask what "constitutes" intelligence (Gardner, 1993: 15).

This discussion begins, then, with a summary examination and brief critique of Howard Gardner's pioneering work on multiple intelligences. Following this look at Gardner's ideas, I present a discussion of the whole language approach to teaching language and literacy: First, because considerable confusion surrounds the whole language movement; second, because it offers a powerful theoretical basis for the teaching of literacies; and third, because it is particularly well suited to incorporating and welcoming "difference" in the classroom.

The Challenge of Multiple Intelligences

> Most of the best people working in these fields [cognitive and behavioral psychology, learning theory] believe that human intelligences are multiple, and that even 'ordinary people,' as measured by the narrow [intelligence] tests we have, are capable—in rich, challenging, nonthreatening environments—of extraordinary feats of intellectual or creative activity. We see just this, in fact, every day in our best workplaces, though too infrequently in our schools and colleges. (Ted Marchese interviewing John Abbott: 5)

Perhaps one of the biggest mistakes that traditional educational systems have made is to assume that all learners learn in the same ways and that intelligence is some sort of single, identifiable entity that can be measured. This kind of ill-conceived generalization is the kind of thinking that grows out of grossly over bureaucratized systems like the American Educational System in which human beings become reduced to categories based on standardized test scores and grade point averages. Unfortunately, such standardization continues to garner powerful support from people like William Bennett, Chester Finn and Pat Buchanan. Howard Gardner, committed to the necessity of reforming the standard educational system, describes this standardized school as follows:

> There is a basic set of competences, and a core body of knowledge, which every individual in our society should master. Some individuals are more able than others, and can be expected to master this knowledge more rapidly. Schools should be set up in such a way to ensure that the most gifted can move to the top and that the greatest number of individuals will achieve basic knowledge as efficiently as possible. For that reason, there should be the same curriculum for all students, the same methods of teaching, and the same "standardized" methods of assessment. Students, teachers, administrators, school districts, states, and even the whole nation should be judged in terms of the efficiency and effectiveness with which these common standards are achieved. Paying attention to individual differences is at best a luxury, at worst a dangerous deviation from essential educational priorities. (69)

Obviously, anyone subscribing to the basic tenets of critical pedagogy or a whole language approach would have difficulty in this "standard" school system. But that problem aside for the moment, let us briefly examine some of the concepts and research that argue against the standardization of schools, curricula, methods of teaching, and testing. Both psycholinguistic research and research in cognitive psychology suggest that, far from being able to measure and talk about an individual's *I*ntelligence *Q*uotient, we need to revise our thinking: individuals appear to have "multiple intelligences" or various cognitive domains. For example, Howard Gardner and his associates have identified "seven intelligences" as follows:

1. "Linguistic intelligence is the kind of ability exhibited in its fullest form, perhaps, by poets."
2. "Logical-mathematical intelligence, as the name implies, is logical and mathematical ability, as well as scientific ability."
3. Spatial intelligence is the ability to form a mental model of a spatial world and to be able to maneuver and operate using that model. This would include "sailors, engineers, surgeons, sculptors, and painters. . . ."
4. "Musical intelligence" is exemplified in people like Leonard Bernstein, Mozart, Miles Davis. . . .

5. "Bodily-kinesthetic intelligence is the ability to solve problems or to fashion products using one's whole body, or
parts of the body." This would be exemplified in "danc-
ers, athletes, surgeons, and craftspeople."

And last, we have "two forms of personal intelligence":

6. "Interpersonal intelligence is the ability to understand
other people: what motivates them, how they work, how
to work cooperatively with them." This might be exemplified in "salespeople, politicians, teachers, clinicians, and
religious leaders."
7. "Intrapersonal intelligence . . . is a capacity to form an
accurate, veridical model of oneself and to be able to use
that model to operate effectively in life" (Gardner, 1993:
8–9).

Having cited Gardner's seven intelligences, let me immediately point out that his is a theoretical position at a relatively
early stage of development. Likewise, psycholinguists continue
to argue for and against the concept that there are specific
language domains (syntactic vs. semantic) as opposed to a general cognitive domain. Considering the fact that many of these
positions continue to be hotly debated, we need not (should
not) accept Gardner's (or anyone else's) definitions or categories as fixed and agreed upon. Gardner himself is careful
to point out that his list of seven intelligences is "a prelimi-
nary" one and that each item on the list can be "subdivided"
(1993: 9).

What is important for this discussion, however, is my belief
that the following are reasonable assumptions: (1) human beings have multiple intelligences (though I suspect we will never
be successful in isolating these intelligences as discrete enti-
ties), and most of us are more "intelligent" in some given categories than in others; (2) Gardner's definitions offer a beginning point for discussing multiple intelligences in some specific
ways; (3) Because a theory of multiple intelligence dismisses
reductivist notions of intelligence by embracing intellectual
diversity, it also offers additional support for the embracing
of various dialects and Discourse systems as legitimate (though

by no means exclusive) modes through which various people express their intelligences; and (4) A theory of multiple intelligences works well with a whole language approach to teaching by virtue of the whole language emphasis on students' individual learning processes and collaborative learning activities.

Now, in some ways, none of this may appear very earth shaking. For years educators have been talking about people having different learning styles (Myers and McCaulley, 1985; Pittenger, 1993). But generally speaking, earlier discussions of learning styles have referred to immutable categories: i.e., Joan learns best when the situation includes a high degree of interpersonal interaction and a movement from global to more discrete elements of whatever is being learned; Michael learns best through verbal explanation from a mentor who then guides him step by step through the elements of whatever is to be learned; Jane learns best when she is independently and actively involved in trying to do whatever is being learned, making mistakes and learning from the mistakes with minimal aid of a mentor, while Tommy becomes quickly frustrated by his mistakes and needs considerable assistance from a mentor both to maintain his motivation and in order to learn from mistakes. . . . Of course, these descriptions make some sense for some learners, but the problem has been that, in the past, we have generalized from the information about learning styles and often assumed that the description of Joan's or Tommy's learning style is accurate *regardless of what is being learned and the developmental stage at which it is being learned.*

Gardner's discussion of multiple intelligences suggests that individuals will have different learning styles, make different demands on teacher-mentors, depending on what it is they are trying to learn and which of their multiple intelligences are (innately?) most advanced or fully developed (Gardner, 1993: 45). Even so, while I believe his ideas are important, overgeneralizing from his discrete categories may cause some potentially serious confusions. It is my own feeling that Gardner's greatest contribution is that he entirely disrupts the already shaky ground of a theory of general intelligence and throws the entire notion of "measurable" intelligence into disrepute. Indeed, as we develop sub-categories of Gardner's seven intelligences, one must begin to question why it is we categorize at all.

Let me use myself as an example here. Learning to read and write (and of course, to speak and listen) were natural and easy for me: I was immersed in a broad range of language activities from an early age, read before beginning school, just seemed to be able to compose at a very early age (third grade), and seemed to get better as the years went on. At the same time I appeared to have these abilities at early ages, I actually did very little reading or writing because I had discovered no personally rewarding reasons for doing so. Writing was a meaningless chore and reading was something I did when I had to: either activity was quickly sacrificed to playing baseball or hockey or just hanging out.

Most of the reading and writing that was demanded of me in school involved rote activities firmly embedded in a skills/drills curriculum. The high school my parents sent me to was carefully tracked according to IQ, and my parents were surprised and confused when I tested into the *D* track (*A* was the elite track, *B* slightly less so, and so on). Of course, I didn't care at all: this was, after all, school, and therefore not very important to me one way or the other. Problems occurred immediately, especially for my teachers and my parents when I began to perform better than I was "supposed to" for someone in the *D* track. At the first parent-teacher conference, my mother questioned why I had received grades in the mid 80's on English and mathematics when I had gotten much higher grades on all my tests. The teacher explained that kids in *D* "couldn't" get grades above the mid 80's. Of course, I was not the only student who had fouled up the tracking system, but instead of the school facing the absurdity of the situation, they simply agreed that I and a few others had been "mistracked." I was moved up to track *B* where I might reasonably get the higher grades I had already been getting. There was discussion of moving me up to *A*, but I successfully argued against this idea because I knew the kinds of academic pressure put on the *A* students and wanted no part of it. Many other students in the lower tracks, I might add, consciously kept their performances mediocre to avoid being moved up to the higher tracks and the added work load and pressure.

I distinctly remember paying little attention to either school or teachers until about eleventh grade at which time I began to enjoy both reading and writing because a teacher with good sense had us reading and discussing "real" literature at the same time he had us regularly engaged in what is now called "freewriting" and other expressive forms of writing. Apparently having a high degree of "linguistic intelligence," all of this came rather easily and naturally to me. I learned by being immersed in the "whole" of language processes, receiving helpful feedback rather late in the process when I began to recognize the need to hone these linguistic abilities. Likewise, sports ability came naturally as I learned first through immersion in the whole and later, when need and desire came together, I honed my skills with the help of coaches and practice of finer skills. But while this suggests a high degree of "kinesthetic intelligence" in Gardner's scheme, it does not show itself at all in two other activities that demand considerable physical coordination. When it comes to using tools, for example, I am inept. Putting a barbecue grill together is, for me, a major project; plumbing is an impossibility. A wrench and a hammer work equally well for me: i.e., not very well.

In terms of Gardner's "musical intelligence," my own experience offers the need for further qualification. Having been immersed in listening to music from a very early age, I have become an avid, some would say obsessed, listener: I own over 600 cd's ranging in style from classical music, traditional and progressive jazz, to hard and alternative rock. At a performative level I sing reasonably well and can improvise vocally. But when it comes to playing guitar, the kinesthetic intelligence that serves me well in sports seems to disappear as well as the intuitive ability that functions when I sing. Playing even the simplest new riff on the guitar costs me hours of practice *with continual assistance* from a mentor/teacher who shows me what I'm doing wrong.

Mathematics has never made much sense to me, but I perform well on standardized math tests. Maps and compasses are, for me, works of art bearing no relationship to the world in which I live.

It is unnecessary to continue these personal examples. While one might argue that my multiple intelligences have been perverted through some kind of attack of "intelligence schizophrenia," I suspect that my examples bear similarities to the learning experiences of many others.

Again, given the basically theoretical nature of any discussion of multiple intelligences, and especially given the fact that it is probably a mistake to see Gardner's list as anything other than a beginning point to aid in a description of the concept, we would make a serious error to decide to rigidly shape learning activities primarily in terms of his list. In fact to do so would simply result in another kind of standardization. On the other hand, it seems perfectly reasonable to use the list as an informal descriptor to help us think about how some of our students approach different kinds of learning activities. And I would further argue that the complexities that abound in the area of examining an individual's varying cognitive abilities and learning styles make qualitative assessment of student learning all the more important and necessary (especially in our classrooms) as opposed to the large, general, quantifiable assessments that often seem to preoccupy education in this country (Courts and McInerney: 1993).

But at this point, I would like to move from the discussion of multiple intelligences to a discussion of some of the teaching methods that have been associated with the whole language approach as we examine the ways in which they might be best modified to meet the challenge posed by students who appear to exhibit different abilities (learning styles, learning needs) in different areas.

A Look at the Whole Language Movement

Learning itself is liberating if it makes the learner more powerful, but the learner must also be in control of the power. We can't liberate learners from the laws of physics, but we can help them use their energy effectively. We can't liberate them from social responsibility, but we can help them to get the most from the social community. We can't liberate pupils from the need to work hard to learn, but we can liberate them from useless drills and drudgery. Ultimately, whole language teachers seek to free the minds and creative energies of pupils for the greatest gains in their intellectual, physical, and social development. (Goodman, 1992: 360)

Many teachers who have been involved with the whole language movement are familiar with the very fine work of people like

Nancy Atwell, Donald Graves, Jerome Harste, and Kenneth Koch, to name just a few of the many now publishing in this area. And to the extent that readers are familiar with some of these authors and practitioners, they are also familiar with the nature of writers' workshops, readers' workshops, non-traditional systems of assessment (student portfolios, taped conferences, videotaping students in class), and so on. Constance Weaver characterizes the whole language approach to teaching in general as follows: "To facilitate learning, teachers need to provide a climate that fosters student ownership; sufficient time for sustained engagement in significant activities; concrete and constructive response, based on the expectation of eventual success; structure that facilitates individual decision making and commitment; and a supportive community that includes both peers and the teacher as co-learners" (371).

But as one who relies on the whole language approach in my own teaching and as one who teaches potential and in-service teachers about whole language and its classroom implications, I have become increasingly aware of the tremendous confusion that surrounds any discussion about whole language, and I am increasingly convinced that the confusion arises from the fact that many practitioners of (and perhaps some who write about) whole language are confused about just exactly what it is they are talking/writing about. Some whole language advocates even go so far as to suggest that some other term be substituted for "whole language" in order to avoid some of the confusion. Such feelings grow out of a belief that "the term had outlived its usefulness since it was frequently misused and misunderstood, and the term itself carried with it significant political baggage" (Strickland and Strickland: 17). At least for the time being, however, I will continue to use the term.

But one immediate confusion, especially given the nature of this book, should be confronted immediately. It is not my contention that a whole language approach to teaching is, in and of itself, "liberating" in the sense that most critical educators use the word. It is my contention that the whole language approach, because of its potential for liberating the individual's learning of and use of literacies, works well *in conjunction with* a critical or liberatory pedagogy. It is particularly important in the context of this book because whole language approaches honor linguistic diversity.

But many other "confusions" are less easy to confront. Just for example, people reading the Summer 1995 issue of the *American Educator* published by the American Federation of Teachers would find themselves seriously confused about a variety of issues I've been discussing. The issue, titled "Learning to Read: Schooling's First Mission" is edited by Elizabeth McPike who explains that the whole language movement "had done a terrible disservice to the children whose lives depend on the mastery of" decoding skills by reducing "decoding to an incidental place in the reading curriculum" (6). She further asserts that "the research is resoundingly clear" on the need to teach phonics as the foundation for reading instruction (6). Aside from the fact that the *resounding clarity* McPike mentions can only result from an incredibly selective reading of research, after reading the entire issue one is left with the sense that the whole language movement applies primarily to grades one–three and is based primarily on some obsessive anti-phonics position. Of course, article after article relies on vague references to "science" to support highly debatable conclusions, but one of the most incredible articles in this collection ("The Missing Foundation in Teacher Education" by Louisa Cook Moats: 9,43–51) argues that teachers do not have enough "linguistic" knowledge to teach reading (phonics) and spelling. While a sophisticated definition of *linguistics* might make such an argument reasonable, this author is concerned that teachers know more about the following: how to find an example of a "bound root" or "derivational suffix"; how to differentiate between syllables and morphemes; how to identify the amount of "speech sounds" in a word (speech sounds? whose speech?); how to identify "consonant digraphs"; how to identify the "six common syllable types in English"; and so on (46). Nary a mention of syntax or dialect; never a moments' concern as to how such "knowledge" would help teachers work with students who are having difficulty learning to read. It is interesting, however, to note that the teachers who did so poorly on the test that Moats gave them are all, presumably, skilled readers. Don't you wonder how that occurred?

At any rate, even a cursory reading of this magazine would make it clear that the whole language movement is subject to serious confusions. It is little wonder that teachers and parents are confused when "scholars" are apparently so willing to misrepresent such complex educational issues.

But even writers and educators who appear drawn toward some central aspects of whole language, like Lisa Delpit (1986, 1988, 1992) and Catherine Walsh (1991), appear critical of it at times.

Although Delpit does not explicitly mention whole language, she appears to associate "process approaches" with teachers who refuse to teach students their writing "skills": She asserts that *some* "radical or progressive teachers of literacy" are "refusing to teach . . . the superficial features (e.g., grammar, form, style) of dominant Discourses." She goes on to say that these teachers "seek instead to develop literacy solely within the language and style of the students' home Discourse" (1992: 300). And in an earlier, related article, she writes: "Of course, there is nothing inherent in the writing-process approach itself which mitigates against students' acquiring standard literacy skills; many supporters of the approach do indeed concern themselves with the technicalities of writing in their own classrooms. However, writing-process advocates often give the impression that they view the direct teaching of skills to be restrictive to the writing process at best, and at worst, politically repressive to students already oppressed by a racist educational system. Black teachers, on the other hand, see the teaching of skills to be essential to their students' survival" (1986: 383).

Aside from the fact that Delpit appears to characterize all black teachers in opposition to the process approach and white teachers as, generally, progressivists who care only about a student's "voice," the central point of the article is that the liberal process-approach people don't listen to the minority teachers and this causes "the minority teachers [to] retreat from these 'progressive' settings grumbling among themselves" (1986: 384). In fairness to Delpit, however, she is walking a fine line in this article and is clearly not arguing for some mindless skill and drill orientation: i.e., "we must insist on 'skills' *within the context of* critical and creative thinking" (1986: 384). My major response to the article, however, would be this: white or black, progressive or conservative, process-oriented or not, some teachers do and say foolish things, often with good intentions. But given that many of my professional acquaintances are process-oriented teachers and most use some version of Atwell's mini-lessons to help students in skill areas, I'm left a little confused by Delpit's references to this progressive group of process-oriented teachers who ignore skills entirely.

Another liberatory educator, Catherine Walsh criticizes process approaches, including whole language, when she suggests that whole language approaches do not encourage students "to question lived realities nor are these realities examined within the context of dominant and dominated relations" (111). This criticism suggests to me that Walsh believes that a whole language approach to teaching necessarily excludes the critical examination of ideological issues in the students' lives, and yet, I see nothing in the underlying principles of the whole language approach to teaching that would preclude such an examination. In fact, I find it hard to understand how a high degree of involvement with students' reading and writing processes could avoid such issues. But my major point here is this: it appears to me that both Delpit and Walsh may be confusing what *some* teachers do or do not do in their classrooms with the essentials of the whole language approach to teaching. In terms of my earlier comments distinguishing among some teachers' classroom *practices*, a whole language *approach* to teaching, and learning *theory*, it appears to me that both Walsh and Delpit are critiquing some teachers' idiosyncratic practices as though they define and represent the approach. I agree with their criticisms, but I don't believe that the problems they cite are inherent in a whole language approach.

More generally, for some educators, whole language is defined by certain generalized methods: writers' workshops; readers' workshops; collaborative learning. For others it is defined by an acceptance of very specific student activities that were not previously deemed acceptable: invented spellings; acceptance of reading miscues that evidence students who are reading for meaning rather than to perform a decoding of sound-symbol relationships. For others it represents the potential abdication of teacher authority and direction, a Rousseauean nightmare of unabridged freedom for students, an irresponsible attitude toward any notion of standards or correctness (Field and Jardine, 1994). Yet others choose to characterize it as just another term for Outcomes-based Education (OBE) and associate it with moral decay (Schlafly, 1993). Even conservative columnist George F. Will (1995) gets into the act, contributing to the confusion by quoting Heather MacDonald, "a contributing editor of the Manhattan Institute's City Journal," who says: "The multiculturalist writing classroom is a workshop on racial and sexual oppression. Rather than studying possessive pronouns, students are learning how language silences women and blacks." Not only that, educators are subjecting students to a "growth model" of education, "an indigestible stew of 1960's liberationist zeal, 1970's deconstructionist nihilism, and 1980's multicultural proselytizing." Obviously, this is pretty serious stuff we are discussing. The issue is so serious that the California State Legislature is considering mandating the adoption of spelling books in the public schools—perhaps one of the most unique responses to the so-called "literacy problem" that I've ever encountered.

Indeed, the degree of confusion seems so rampant (and, sometimes, willful?) that I am never sure what someone means when, s/he says, as I did in the beginning of this article, "I support the whole language movement and try to implement the whole language approach in my own teaching." Just by way of example, in a graduate course I taught recently focusing on whole language approaches to teaching multicultural literatures, most of the teachers in the class stated that they used "whole language" in their classrooms. And yet, when I asked them to define what they meant by whole language, serious confusion set in. At the same time, most of them clearly did base their teaching on a whole language foundation, but few were able to explain the fundamental, theoretical underpinnings of the whole language approach. I distributed Ken Goodman's article "Why Whole Language Is Today's Agenda in Education," and many of them found it particularly important because they were feeling isolated in their attempts to implement whole language approaches in their schools. I should also add, as Goodman suggests, those teachers from schools least typical of the white middle-class mainstream were most committed to whole language and the high school teachers were the least committed. But while the article helped them, it did not settle the confusion.

While I agree with much that Ken Goodman wrote in that article, I would add a few qualifications. Yes, the whole language movement is a ground-up movement, and it is being implemented by many excellent teachers. Likewise, Goodman's characterization of the movement and its theoretical foundations are accurate and helpful. But in many of the schools with which I am familiar, particularly the high schools, the teachers who employ a whole language approach often find themselves relatively isolated and sometimes the victims of derision. In addition to this observation, I note one sentence that stands out in Goodman's article: "Whole language has come to mean many things to many groups" (354). And it is this multitude of meanings, confusions over the meaning of *whole language*, if you will, that I want to address here. But please note, this is not in any way intended as a refutation of Goodman's points; rather it is an attempt to further clarify what is sometimes not addressed in discussions of whole language. Goodman provides a powerful description of the ways in which whole language is slowly moving into the nation's schools, but from my own perspective the movement is meeting considerably more resistance than Goodman suggests.

Conservative columnist Cal Thomas provides a clear example of the kinds of confusion (perhaps intentional) that permeates many public discussions of whole language (1996). In this editorial, Thomas essentially defines "whole language" as an anti-phonics approach to teaching initial reading schools—an approach that emphasizes "word recognition taught by associating words and pictures." Essentially blaming his version of "whole language" teaching as the reason that the entire state of California's schools are in such disarray and teaching students so poorly, he sees a return to phonics instruction as the salvation of literacy in the schools. Adding another uninformed insight, he also points out that our nation's schools are by no means "underfunded." One wonders if he would be willing to make that argument openly from within the halls of schools in central Los Angeles, Queens, Chicago, Detroit?

Of course, I make no pretense about being able to affect the thinking of people like Thomas. But because I am a strong supporter of whole language and use the approach in my own teaching, I would like to break down some of the resistance I see among the teachers with whom I work and perhaps offer teachers some ways in which they might help parents understand the nature of a whole language approach to teaching. I am particularly concerned about the resistance that I see among high school teachers. And (with the clear exception of some enlightened freshman composition teachers and educationists) I can't even characterize college teachers as "resisting whole language" since so few even consider the movement to have anything to do with them.

But my major concern at the moment is to examine some of the confusions surrounding the whole language movement. I begin with a brief overview of some of the confusion surrounding the movement and then an explanation of the essentials of the whole language movement so that it won't "mean [so] many things to [so] many groups." Indeed, anything that means too many things means very little.

Before going any further, however, I would like to propose a definition of whole language. Second, I will use that definition to examine some examples of the kinds of confusion I am referring to above. And third, I want to use the definition to exemplify how the theoretical underpinnings of whole language led me into some confused pedagogical practice and, eventually, out of the confusion.

Notes About the Whole Language Approach

1. The whole language approach is an *emerging* philosophical position growing out of cognitive learning theory's descriptions of how human beings at various ages (NOT just early elementary level students) learn language and literacy *and develop* from the initial stages of language and literacy into facile, skilled, literate users of language both as speakers and as writers (C. Weaver: 364–436).

2. As a general approach based on a theory of learning it must not be reduced to a limited set of classroom practices, but it can help those who understand the theoretical underpinnings *generate* classroom methods, *critique* classroom methods, and *change* classroom methods in order to better facilitate their students' learning.

3. Because it is most useful as a system that generates classroom practices and for critiquing the results of those approaches, *it must continue to emerge* as practitioners experiment with the approach and its implications.

4. And finally, as an emerging theory about how human beings learn language and literacy, it simply cannot be viewed

or discussed as a *solution* to teaching language and literacy. (While it is conceivable that there are solutions to help individual learners, it is inconceivable to me, given many years of teaching experience, that there is single solution for all learners. And if there is one, we certainly haven't discovered it yet.)

What Are the Specifics of This Theory?

First and foremost, it is important to stress that, except for the rubric *whole language,* many of the concepts and classroom practices associated with whole language have been around since the mid 1960s and probably long before that if we consider the body of John Dewey's work, particularly *Art As Experience* (Goodman, 1992: 355). Those familiar with John Dixon's *Growth Through English* (first published in 1966), the works of Stephen and Susan Tchudi (over the past 20 years), James Moffett's work over the past 20 years, James Britton's work, the works of Ken and Yetta Goodman . . . already know that "whole language," as an approach, has been *emerging* over the last 30 years (or 80 years if one considers the pioneering work of John Dewey). It is an approach whose underpinnings grow out of research that has been done and is currently being done in the areas of psycholinguistics, sociolinguistics, and cognitive psychology (not to mention anthropology, philosophy, and recent theoretical studies about how readers make meaning of texts). Indeed, it is because the whole language approach has been emerging for at least the last 30 years and the fact that it grows out of such a broad range of disciplines, many of which are relatively new areas of study themselves—it is because of this that it is difficult to define. (But what complex approach to teaching has ever been easy to explain and define?) Furthermore, at the same time that the whole language approach grows out of these important areas of research, it also reflects influences growing out of the liberatory pedagogy movement (Aronowitz and Giroux; Freire; Macedo; McLaren), a movement that strongly supports the importance of empowering learners as active formulators of their own intellectual and psychological growth. Little wonder that confusion exists! Still, remembering that any active theoretical position is in the process of emerging and changing, it is worth the attempt to explain this whole language approach more fully, and perhaps even mitigate some of the confusion.

Theoretical Principles of Whole Language

1. All human beings of all cultures learn their native language by approximately age five and they do so through informal, consistent, highly motivated interaction with caretakers/mediators (Halliday; P. Bloom; Fernald; Petito). In this process, the learners are immersed in normal language interactions (not skills drills). To put it rather simply, a whole language approach views human beings holistically and avoids the artificial fragmenting of learning situations.

2. An integral part of the language-learning process is the sociolinguistic learning that accompanies it: in the process of learning the language and experiencing a broad range of linguistic and social interactions, the child begins to gain a basic kind of cultural literacy, an understanding of the society in which s/he is being raised, while also developing a participatory, constructive role in that society. In a very real sense, the learner not only learns the semantics of the native language but the semantics of the culture (Halliday, 1978).

3. Learners are *constructive, creative participants* who bring as much to a learning situation as they take from it: their *innate* generative ability to *create* a sense of the world is emphasized. Psycholinguistic research, while still sorting through an enormous array of complexities surrounding the language-learning process, clearly rejects behaviorism as a fundamental explanation for language learning and posits the human being as innately capable of *generating* meaning.

4. The learners' natural propensity to explore and make sense of their environment is nurtured. Cognitive psychologists (and most teachers) know that human beings learn best when they want to learn, are interested and involved in the learning experience, and have a strong sense of individual empowerment.

5. Likewise, while human beings can clearly "learn" some things in isolation, much learning, like language acquisition itself, occurs most fruitfully in social settings involving interaction and active involvement on the part of the learner: i.e., the process of language acquisition generalizes to other kinds of learning situations at various other stages in the learners' development. This is directly related to James Gee's distinction between *acquisition* and *learning*.

6. Learning occurs most productively when learners participate in setting goals, identifying objectives, and planning activities. Learners and teachers must work together in a cooperative setting in which power is shared as all work together to create a community. Traditional educational approaches that simply impose preformulated curricula and classroom activities on students ignore individual differences and needs and stifle the generative, constructive possibilities that might facilitate the growth of a genuinely literate public. (Indeed, from a political point of view, a highly restrictive system of education succeeds in disempowering the electorate, causing the people to feel that they have little possibility of effecting any change in anything. Having spent anywhere from 12 to 18 years doing what they have been told to do, memorizing the answers to preformulated questions, it does not occur to them that they can be active in their own lives [Courts, 1991].)

7. The ability to master skills that are a part of larger processes occurs best when the skills are learned in the context of a given process rather than in isolated, fragmented skills exercises: appropriate syntax, narrative structure, punctuation, spelling, etc. are all most efficiently and genuinely learned when the skills are examined and stressed as part of the composing process itself.

8. The creation of various written forms from poetry to personal narrative to the critical essay is essential to helping students successfully and happily understand such literature produced by others. Instead of simply studying what has been longest known and best understood (Samuel Johnson), students create their own articulations and compare these statements of self with what others (classmates, professionals . . .) have produced.

9. Learners use language (reading, viewing, writing, speaking, and listening) as a means of finding out what they themselves mean and as part of a process of gaining an awareness of their own thought processes and problem solving processes. As they become increasingly metacognitive, they begin to use language processes in a *conscious* attempt to establish a relationship between self and other.

10. Critical thinking, deciding what ideas are best and what texts "mean," involves communal negotiation, and thus the

emphasis on self and metacognition in #9 above leads to language uses that emphasize communication with others and active engagement in establishing communal realities (Courts, 1991).

In sum, the whole language approach sees learners as integrated, whole human beings who, through their innate generative abilities and desire to make meaning in and of the world, are in the process of using language to create a conscious self and negotiate a relationship with all that is outside them. And given that this process is more than a little complex, it can hardly be suggested that whole language teachers could reasonably construct classrooms without structure, order, or assessment. Quite the opposite: one of the major challenges facing the whole language teacher is the difficulty of creating learning environments and classroom activities that encourage learners to remain engaged in what can often be a frustrating, even threatening, process—i.e., genuine learning. Of course, the structures and order of the whole language classroom are generally quite different from the more dominant structures of the traditional classroom in which teachers talk and students listen (or at least pretend to). Traditional approaches to structuring classrooms, teaching, and assessment have long been criticized for their ineffectiveness and even destructive nature. The whole language approach, far from ignoring issues of structure and assessment is generating exciting new ideas about structuring classrooms and assessing students' learning. The very essence of the approach welcomes the idea of multiple intelligences *because* it focuses, always, on the *growth and performance of the individual students across a whole range* of language activities. Depending on their various strengths and abilities in a given area of performance (reading, writing, critical thinking, creative/analogic/metaphoric thinking), different students will need to be immersed in different learning activities depending on what it is that is being learned/taught.

Whole Language Confusions and Critiques

As I said earlier, one of the values of a whole language approach and a clear understanding of its theoretical ground is the power this provides one in critiquing one's own or another's teaching—not, of course, simply to be critical, but in order to help teachers become more conscious of the effects their methods have on their students and to provide constructive modifications of those methods. The following situations provide an opportunity to see both the kinds of confusions that sometimes occur in "whole language" teaching and the ways in which whole language can serve as a critique that might be used by those of us who attempt to teach in terms of its theoretical base. The names of the teachers are obviously fictional, and I've changed specifics just enough to make it impossible, I hope, for anyone to identify any individuals, but each of the situations accurately represents a real occurrence.

Mr. Smith, claiming to be using a whole language approach with his second grade, is dictating a paragraph to his young students as they dutifully copy the sentences in their "journals." He is doing this in order to help them develop their listening skills, and he is consciously avoiding the "baby" language of basal readers and the complicated rules of phonics systems. The paragraph is about a boy who wants to buy a pizza but ends up having to make his own pizza. The first sentence he dictates is as follows: "James said, 'I am hoping to use my pizza certificate to make my purchase.'" If students have questions about spelling or punctuation, Mr. Smith willingly interrupts the dictation to provide a "mini-lesson," engaging the students in a discussion of the sentence, the spelling (phonics) rules for a given word, and rules of punctuation. Next, the dictation continues until the paragraph is completed, and students now practice "reading" the paragraph in preparation for oral performances of the reading. The lesson appears to have successfully incorporated the processes of speaking, listening, reading, writing, *and* the "skills" of spelling and punctuation. Later, perhaps, students will interview their parents in order to gather enough different pizza recipes to create a pizza cookbook. Finally, they will make pizzas, learn about kitchen safety, measuring units like cups, ounces, teaspoons, degrees Fahrenheit. . . .

In many ways, there is nothing terribly wrong here, and Mr. Smith appears to be trying to implement some of the things he learned by reading Atwell's *In the Middle*. But he's gotten a few things mixed up and they are important things. Clearly he has forgotten or missed the importance of having students engage in authentic language activities. By dictating the paragraph, he succeeds in "modeling" a standard school paragraph, but forgets the importance of students using their own language to create and communicate issues that are of importance to them. He further forgets that this kind of rote copying does little to teach students anything about how to write. As far as writing goes, the emphasis is clearly on skills practice divorced from the act of constructive meaning making on the parts of the writers. The follow-up pizza activity makes perfectly good sense, but the first part of the activity intended to develop students' writing and listening abilities is highly questionable.

Ms. Jones, also claiming to be using a whole language approach to teaching her first graders to read, is having them "write" their own stories. She is not concerned that some of them use almost no vowels or that their sentences are not standard English. She wants them to experiment with their own language and their own narrative abilities. Although she is concerned that when Tommy's "invented spellings" bear no discernible relationship to the words in the story he says he is writing, she doesn't want to stifle his creativity in any way. Consequently, she is reluctant to talk with him about the most rudimentary sound-symbol relationships, and finds herself confused about how to help this learner move beyond his present level of literacy. She knows that teaching "phonics" *per se*, especially as a central method of teaching reading is a waste of time, but she also knows that Tommy does not appear to be developing as a writer/reader or to have a firm sense of the essential nature/purpose of printed language.

This is an interesting case because, Ms. Jones finally decided to explicitly work with Tommy on sound-symbol relationships, though she did so with guilt, feeling that somehow she was violating what she had learned about teaching reading and writing as a whole language teacher. She had forgotten the importance of a mediator in the learning process: yes, language is learned by all people by the age of five, and yes, many children learn to read (and sometimes) write before going to school because of extensive home interactions focusing on print literacy. But this happens because there are mediators (teachers) present—usually parents—who intervene and provide information and help when the learner is stumped. No teacher can refuse to mediate, refuse to help the learner when help is essential, and any theory that supported such a teaching stance would be mighty strange indeed.

Fortunately for Tommy, Ms. Jones also realized that his problem went considerably beyond sound-symbol relationships and phonics. Her understanding of whole language theory helped her to see that Tommy really didn't understand what reading, writing and print were all about. In many ways, he was like the Appalachian boy, Donny (Chapter 3), who had no idea of print/language relationships. Of course, having come from a home environment in which print literacy was virtually non-existent, this was not too surprising. Consequently, Ms. Jones and an aid began spending a considerable amount of time reading to Tommy as he followed along, interrupting occasionally to discuss a specific word or phrase, trying to help Tommy develop a sense of what print and reading is all about. I should also note, however, that Ms. Jones was too sophisticated about language and reading to revert to trying to "hook" Tommy on phonics, an act that she knew would simply cement the confusion he was already experiencing.

Mr. Brown, claiming to be using a whole language approach, has his eighth grade students write persuasive essays about any topic they choose, five paragraphs in length: the first paragraph indicates the exact issue to be argued; the next three argue the issue (first presenting the counter-arguments, second refuting those arguments, and third, making the correct argument); and the final paragraph reiterates the previous four. Next the students "peer-edit" the essays, focusing primarily on whether or not the essay fits the five-paragraph format and then on spelling and punctuation; after this, they "revise" (i.e., *correct* the mistakes). Finally, each student reads his/her essay aloud to the class, thus incorporating the writing, reading, speaking, and listening processes in a given activity. Mr. Brown would like to incorporate more creative writing activities (he knows his students are bored by what they are doing), but he feels constrained by the comments made by the high school teachers who assert that the "license" inherent in the whole language movement has created a "generation" of students who cannot write a standard essay with proper punctuation and correct spelling (unlike the mythical generations of students who came before and produced beautifully wrought essays).

Unfortunately, Mr. Brown operates in contradiction to his best instincts. He wants to implement his own version of writers' workshop in his classroom, using all that he has learned and likes about giving students the opportunity to discover and develop their own interests in writing, having them discover their own writing processes and learn ways of improving those processes, but he is under pressure from the high school teachers who have decided to blame him for the "decline in student literacy that has been caused by this whole language stuff and giving students so much freedom." He is unaware of the fact that the mythical golden age of literacy cited by the high school teachers is just that—mythical. He is also unaware that the weak literacy skills of the students the other teachers complain about can generally be attributed to the "skills and drills" emphasis that characterizes what is generally going on in the elementary and middle school he is teaching in. He has allowed the unfounded charges of other teachers to stop him from following his own professional instincts, and as a result, neither he nor his students are satisfied. And yet, in fairness to him, it is very important to remember how isolated some teachers become when they attempt to create change in systems that have long been successfully resistant to change and use false arguments to argue against and disparage change.

Ms. Gray uses the whole language approach with her advanced twelfth grade English class. Her students are writing research papers on *Macbeth*. She believes that she is implementing a "process" approach because the students move through the following process: each must find three books in the library on *Macbeth*, create at least three "note cards" correctly quoting and footnoting appropriate material from the texts, and a correct bibliographic notation for each. Each student must then produce a four to six page research paper. These papers are peer-edited in class, but the focus of the editing is on the correct form of the footnotes, punctuation, and usage. Students are encouraged to "share their research" with one another in small "literary exploration" groups and the papers are collected into a class publication on *Macbeth*. Like Mr. Brown, she would like to involve her students in more varied kinds of literary and creative writing activities, but she feels constrained by the demands of the New York State Regent's exam, the pressure on her students to achieve high scores on the SAT exam, and the demands of first year college writing courses.

Ms. Gray is caught in several traps. First, her concern with students' performance on gatekeeping exams and the SAT's causes her to teach toward those exams. Second, though she likes the idea of whole language, she does not fully believe that a whole language approach will prepare her students to succeed on standardized exams. Third, and most important, Ms. Gray is confused about what comprises a whole language approach, and no one has really helped her to understand how she might use such an approach in her own classroom. This is a particularly important point in this kind of a discussion because the whole language movement, like most "change" in education, seems to be expected to take place without administrators and school systems providing much support to help teachers learn about it.

Mr. Pool's whole language approach immerses his tenth graders in extensive independent reading and writing activities. The classroom is filled with paperbacks and comfortable "reading stations." The "writer's station" provides students with a quiet place to work on their independent writing projects. Students are free to help one another when asked, but for the most part, no two people are ever working together on the same thing. In an attempt to encourage students to discover and pursue their own strengths as fully as possible, no large-group activities are imposed on the students. He believes that the literary canon has deprived students of reading important literature by women and minorities; he further believes that the only way to empower his students is to give them complete freedom of choice in their reading and writing activities. Mr. Pool is available for individual conferences whenever a student asks for assistance. He sees himself primarily as a guide and as a classroom source.

Mr. Pool's dilemma is not a terribly unusual one. Because he sees the value of one set of methodological approaches, readers' and writers' workshops and emphasis on students' working independently, he has excluded other important kinds of classroom interactions and activities. While the whole language approach clearly supports the kinds of workshops Mr. Pool employs, I see nothing in the theory to suggest that students could not also profitably read a given text, on occasion, and talk and write about it. Indeed, if students are going to engage in the negotiation of meaning, they must participate in such activities. And one might well ask, if all the work is going to be primarily independent, why would we bother to gather in classrooms. The point here is that the whole language approach does not exclude any constructive learning activities. And if it appears to, then the whole language approach must be modified (remember, it is an *emerging* approach).

However one wishes to characterize the scenarios above, it is my position that none of them helps much in defining a whole language approach to teaching. In a very real sense, each scenario represents various degrees of (mis)understanding of what the whole language movement is about. But in fairness to the teachers, each vignette pictures a teacher who is attempting to change what s/he has traditionally done in the classroom. Unfortunately, teachers often find themselves attempting such change with little outside help or support, and the resulting confusion is easily understandable. As is so often the case, as good ideas move into the field of education, they are implemented as "methods" before they are explored as theories about human learning processes. Philosophies and theories are reduced to and defined in terms of methodologies (for example, "Whole language means the avoidance of phonics and an emphasis on invented spellings"), rather than being used as generative bases upon which methods might be founded, critiqued, and revised. And it is not unusual for well-intended administrators to mandate changes that they themselves do not fully understand, without providing funding for in-service workshops to help their teachers explore and implement such changes. Consequently, teachers often find themselves attempting such change in isolation, with no one to talk to about their various degrees of success and failure.

On the other hand, it is essential that teachers experiment with classroom methods; otherwise nothing will ever change. But when the experimentation is done in the belief that the *new method will solve all problems*, then the experiment is doomed to failure. Almost everything I've ever tried for the first time (and second time and third time) in a classroom has misfired in some way, sometimes seriously. Because I have ways of critiquing what I try, however, I am able to modify the method, slowly trying to find the best way to work with my students and help them learn whatever it is we are working on. But if I do not see myself involved in this kind of process of self-critiquing and change, then I may "blame the *approach that helped me generate* the methods," and go back to whatever I was doing before, happy with the excuse that at least I tried. And given how much any kind of change is resisted in schools, this often appears to be what is happening: halfheartedly try a new method, watch it fail, and go back to business as usual. Given a lack of administrative support for major school change, I suspect that the only way through such a dilemma is for teachers to create their own support and in-service training groups: here teachers can discuss their experiments, exchange critiques and ideas for modification, and help each other keep up the considerable energy that is necessary to do this kind of teaching. (Of course, this is exactly what many fine teachers have been doing for years.)

But enough about other teachers and their confusions. It's time I used myself as an example.

In an attempt to implement a reader/writer workshop in an upper-level English course we teach in Adolescent Literature, my colleague Dr. Joan Burke and I worked together to create a course that would no longer refer to the work of Romano, Atwell, et al., but that would actually do what these teachers and authors suggest. Our experiment was by no means a total failure, but it helped us to understand better the complexities and pitfalls that are inherent in the process of "growing into whole language."

Having decided to focus the core readings on multicultural literature dealing with the adolescent experience, we also provided a selected list of additional readings from which students could choose to select their independent readings. We would structure our courses so that any given class meeting might include some mix like the following: the instructor reads the class a few poems dealing with the topic of adolescence followed by open discussion of and reaction/response to the poems, followed by a 20-minute independent writing period (all in-class writing would be in the students' journals). The second half of the 80-minute period might be followed with a few student presentations based on one of the independent readings s/he had chosen.

In addition to these kinds of activities, we also had the students form small groups, each of which would be responsible for presenting the class with a presentation on one of the core readings. Although these presentations were very open-ended in terms of what students might choose to do—ranging from dramatic improvisations to activities that actively engaged the rest of the class in a discussion of the novel or related issues— they generally focused on some informal attempt by the group to "teach" the novel they were responding to. Although students were required to write several papers in the course, and while a few chose to write relatively traditional critical essays, many chose to write creative responses to the core readings. And all the students were encouraged to write some poems and/or short fiction. Of course, all writing was peer-edited and discussed in small and large groups. Much of the creative writing was performed orally by the writers as part of the "open readings" we had built into the course structure.

Having spent months structuring and restructuring the course, choosing readings, creating activities, discussing means of assessing the students' growth . . . we embarked with considerably more trepidation than one might expect of highly experienced teachers (my colleague, Dr. Joan Burke, had taught high school for more than 15 years). The trepidation was well founded: but not because all of this failed or because students disliked the course or felt that they had not learned. Indeed, the open-ended, written student evaluations of the course indicated a high degree of satisfaction and enjoyment as well as some insightful criticisms. (As Stephen Tchudi said to me 25 years ago, "Sometimes I wonder if students give us strong course evaluations because everything else they are experiencing in classrooms is godawful.") But it is the criticisms that I want to focus on now, both those that came from the students and those that Dr. Burke and I had from our own observations.

Students complained that we often gave them too little time to work on their writing in class, that being told NOW is writing time didn't work for them, that they were sometimes distracted by other students talking with one another about a piece of writing or by noise in the hallway. Small groups often found it difficult to meet often enough as a group outside of class; some members didn't pull their own weight; they were sometimes confused about the objectives of their class presentations. And several students noted that the quality of peer-editing depended entirely on who did the peer-editing.

From my own and Dr. Burke's points of view, we had overly fragmented the class meetings, perhaps trying to get too many things "done"; students would just begin to get involved in one activity (creative writing, for example), when we would switch gears and move them into a discussion of one of the readings. Our fundamental mistake, though we had foreseen this as a possibility, was in not recognizing the significant differences that exist for high school students who are in a class five days per week, where regular changes and variation in activities are necessary to keep the interest levels high, as opposed to students who are in class two to three times per week for periods of 50 or 80 minutes. Activities that might fit nicely into the five-day week became confused and confusing in the college setting. Likewise, in our zeal to implement "real" readers' and writers' workshops, we mistakenly assumed that our students would want class time in which to do independent reading, and we failed to anticipate the somewhat artificial setting we had created for their writing. More generally, we both made the mistake of trying to implement "methods" without fully recognizing the unhappy mix of these methods with our environment, class schedules, and the needs/desires/developmental levels of our students.

But as I said at the very outset of this chapter, the power of a good theoretical foundation and a solid general approach, like whole language, is that it offers the basis for generating *and critiquing* what we do in classrooms in order to make more productive changes. But first we had to see that we had been overly concerned with implementing methods we had read about and come to realize that our changes needed to be based on real students and real learning experiences. And changes we made, just a few of which are as follows: we significantly reduced fragmentation of class time and tried to integrate the relationship between activities in a given class meeting much more carefully and avoided more than two activities per class meeting: i.e., peer-editing on a given paper is followed by discussion of the ideas in the drafts of the paper leading into a discussion of the novel being written about. We engage in large-group discussions of selected student drafts to help students learn approaches to peer-editing. In order to clarify objectives for small group presentations on novels, we schedule formal conferences with small groups one week in advance of the presentations: i.e., members of small groups are aided in developing strategies to engage the class in discussion of a given work, structuring discussion questions, discovering related poetry or videotapes that might move the discussion beyond the given novel. We require individuals in each small group to write evaluations of the group's preparation and performance. We provide a list of broadly varied writing activities (including many ideas for fiction/poetry) for all the works read in the course, but we still encourage individual choice for those who work best independently. We encourage students who find large group discussion difficult and personally threatening to keep personal journals in which they respond to class discussion of the literature. We schedule individual conferences outside of class meetings; identify given class meetings for independent reading, but do not require students to do the reading in the classroom. We schedule midterm class evaluation to get student feedback and ideas related to possible changes that might be made for the second half of semester. We give students regular opportunities to discuss scheduling of independent reading days, paper due-dates. . . .

But what is the point of this kind of example? At least in part, it is this. Both Dr. Burke and I have studied and taught about whole language approaches to teaching. We have implemented activities in our courses based on whole language. We have structured writing courses significantly influenced by Atwell's work. I teach a course in Language and Literacy that not only engages students in a study of the whole language approach and its implications, but is essentially structured in terms of the whole language approach. So we should have known better, right? No—not right! Whatever it may look like to an outsider, we know that we had to conduct the experiment before we could know what we needed to know better about! And equally important, we were able to support each other and work together to make the necessary modifications. We both felt that our observations and the helpful critiques and evaluations offered by our students allowed us each to create a much improved Adolescent Literature course.

Up to this point, most of the discussion in this chapter has focused on the whole language approach to teaching and the theory of multiple intelligences. But in a very real sense, the discussion has yet to articulate the liberatory center that it suggested in earlier chapters. In fact, I strongly suspect that some criticisms of whole language and process approaches, like those generated by Delpit and Walsh, offer well-founded cautions. Any teaching approach that becomes obsessed with *process* contains the potential to forget that there are *reasons* for engaging in learning processes. From my own perspective, we engage in learning processes because they fulfill personal needs *and* allow us to actively participate in our world. As active participants in our own process of becoming and as constructive agents in the world in which we live, we have the potential to "do" the world instead of simply letting it "do" us!

Following this lead, the next chapter exemplifies a general methodology. It provides examples of classroom activities that are intended to help readers teach students from diverse linguistic and cultural backgrounds at the same time they begin to acquire and critique dialects, Discourses, and difference. And it directly suggests the crossroad at which whole language and border pedagogies meet.

Chapter 5

Walkin' the Walk:
Singing the Voices Electric

Were I to do it again, I would construct my curriculum around the celebration, validation, and critical questioning of the symbolic and expressive forms within the specific cultural practices of the students' street-corner milieu. (McLaren: 232)

Border pedagogy confirms and critically engages the knowledge and experience through which students author their own voices and construct social identities. . . . Such experience has to be both *affirmed and interrogated*. (Aronowitz and Giroux: 128–129. Italics added.)

In an America, particularly in the United States, which is overwhelmingly present every day, in every social, political, cultural economic, psychological way, it's hard not to feel as if you're *confronting* a reality that's so powerful you can't expect it to recognize you. . . . I believe a major part of the way has to do with the consciousness we have of our selves, the language we use (not necessarily only native languages but the consciousness of our true selves at the core of whatever language we use, including English), and our responsible care for and relationships we have with our communities and communal lands. This is the way as Native Americans we will come into being as who we are within the reality of what we face. (Ortiz: 26–27)

Finally! What does all the "stuff" that precedes this chapter actually have to do with teaching? The answers are: (1) quite a lot; and (2) much of it is significantly different from what normally goes on in schools. First and foremost, as the opening quotes to this chapter suggest, the experiences and voices of the students must become central. Students at all levels must be given the opportunity to sing their own songs in their own ways, experimenting with voice and language to make those songs more powerful and more fully articulated. Students' dialects, Discourse systems, out of school experiences, traditions, beliefs, hopes, fears—students lives must become central within the classroom. But this is not enough. If the description for change were to stop here, it would invite proper criticism: celebration of the individual voice, in and of itself, has the potential to isolate students within their own egocentric worlds.

Aronowitz and Giroux properly warn against what I call the Dr. Feel-Good school of teaching which encourages student voices just for the sake of hearing/reading student voices. Under these conditions, when a pedagogical approach focuses "exclusively on issues of dialogue, process, and exchange . . . critical pedagogy comes perilously close to emulating the liberal-progressive tradition in which teaching is reduced to getting students merely to express or assess their own experiences. Teaching collapses in this case into a banal notion of facilitation, and student experience becomes an unproblematic vehicle for self-affirmation and self consciousness. . . . It overprivileges the notion of student voice, and refuses to engage its contradictory nature" (117).

To this last quote, I would add that the line between over privileging the student's voice and allowing it no privilege is not as fine as it sometimes appears. Students and teachers have a right to say/write what they think: this only becomes problematic when teachers feel that they have no right (or responsibility) to confront a student whose speaking/writing is, for example, racist or sexist, vicious and hurtful; likewise, the teacher has a responsibility to help the student who is simply vacuous. But the teacher also has the responsibility to encourage students to voice their experiences and opinions openly so that the opinions and experiences *can be examined, discussed, analyzed, argued about.* And if authentic dialogue is to occur, teachers cannot use their tools of authority (i.e., grades, ridicule) to short-circuit student criticism of the teacher's points of view. Discuss? Argue? Yes. Silence? Fearful acquiescence? No.

It seems obvious to me that, just as consistent, negative criticism of everything students say or write guarantees the angry silence of students, non-critical praise for everything a student produces guarantees little growth. But criticism need not be hostile or negative any more than it needs to be gilded: a *criti-*

cal pedagogy invites careful examination and assessment of everyone's articulations. A sensitive, straightforward classroom dialogue, born in an environment of mutual respect, provides both teachers and learners with the opportunity to transform schools into sites of real learning.

Of course, real learning inherently involves mistake making, but in most schools, making mistakes is to be avoided, at best, or hidden, if you can't avoid it. In a learning-centered classroom, however, students must be helped to realize that their mistakes are a perfectly normal part of the learning process. If I am trying to acquire a new Discourse, I am bound to say and do things that don't "fit": if my mistakes cause me to be ridiculed or punished, I'm likely to retreat from the entire activity. But if my mistakes are viewed by me, my teachers, and my peers as part of the learning process and an indication that I need and deserve some assistance, I will be much more likely to experiment with newness and difference. An overly critical pedagogy creates the silence born of fear. A non-critical pedagogy is a pedagogy that simply doesn't care about what anyone says or writes. And a completely non-critical stance taken toward any and all self-expression disables students by making them think that all ideas, opinions, and performances are equally good. It also creates the likelihood that they will remain in the states of destructive "resistance" that Peter McLaren describes. Growing out of his discussion of Paul Willis's work and the work of Jacques Lacan, McLaren describes students whose lives are directed by a "passion for ignorance": "Ignorance, as part of the very structure of knowledge, can teach us something. But we lack the critical constructs with which to recover that knowledge *which we choose not to know.* Unable to find meaningful knowledge 'out there' in the world of pre-packaged commodities, students resort to random violence or an intellectual purple haze where anything more challenging than the late night news is met with retreat, or despair; and of course, it is the dominant culture that benefits most from this epidemic of conceptual anesthesia. The fewer critical intellectuals around to challenge its ideals, the better" (McLaren: 189).

Not much needs to be added to McLaren's insightful examination of the resistance of many students to the agenda of schools and schooling in America. And while many of those whose "passion for ignorance" motivates their rebellion against or dismissal of school culture are minority students and/or students from lower socioeconomic classes, the description includes students from all walks of life. Indeed, John Ogbu's general body of work suggests that the kind of resistance described by McLaren is central to the culture of many ghetto communities where, for too many of our youth, status and prosperity in the "hood" are achieved through violent crime and the enormous amounts of money to be made through drugs. Consciously or unconsciously, these young people see no possibility for status and prosperity outside the "hood" because the destructive domination of the mainstream culture makes it clear that they do not belong in the mainstream. Staying within the culture of the hood, victimizing one's neighbors, making tremendous amounts of fast money off drug sales—activities that usually lead to an early death—this paradox of self-destructive resistance further confirms the mainstream's domination. Nothing changes and victims victimize victims.

But I believe it is essential for teachers to understand that, although much of Ogbu's commentary is specifically applicable to some black communities, the general abyss he describes can aid us in understanding the psyches of many other students trapped in small towns and city ghettoes, students who see no possibilities for themselves beyond the confines of the neighborhood or small town. The fact that the town appears to be very different from the "hood" does not necessarily alter the sense of confinement, dead-ends, and purposelessness that seem to characterize the worlds of many of the young people in our society. The passion for ignorance is by no means limited in terms of skin color or ethnicity. And the unarticulated despair of many of our young people is readily apparent to almost anyone who has taught in any public school, particularly above the middle school level. I have believed for many years that schools use bells or buzzers to note the beginning and end of class periods in order to awaken everyone from the droning slumber that characterizes so many classrooms. In many schools, much more is learned in the hallways and bathrooms than in the classrooms—though we may not like much of what is learned.

So singing their own songs in their own voices is not enough. Students must also begin to hear *and examine* the songs that others sing; they must be conscious of the fact that they have the power to learn the songs that others sing and that they have the power to critique some of those songs. In order to move beyond a "passion for ignorance," I must first discover the power of *knowing and being able to know*. In order to actively pursue knowing and the process of coming to know, I must be safe enough to make mistakes and learn from them without fear of attack. In order to be anything other than a subject constructed by a dominant mainstream culture that cares not a whit about me, I must come to know the nature of the dominant culture and develop the ability to confront and change it.

And this last sentence raises the importance of memory and counter memory: Our students need to remember that which they know nothing about, especially insofar as that which they cannot remember (know nothing about) has constructed them and the world in which they live. As Stuart Hall says, people "need to understand the languages which they've been taught not to speak. They need to understand and revalue the traditions and inheritances of cultural expression and creativity. And in that sense, the past is not only a position from which to speak, but it is also an absolutely necessary resource. . . ." This "constructed" past "is part of narrative. We tell ourselves [and others] the stories of the parts of our roots in order to come into contact, creatively, with it. So this new kind of ethnicity— the emergent ethnicities—has a relationship to the past, but it is a relationship that is partly through memory, partly through narrative, one that has to be recovered. It is an act of cultural recovery" (Hall: 18-19).

Counter memory means to remember that which counters (challenges) all that has been remembered "for" you by the official rememberers. And perhaps more importantly, it means to remember all that has been carefully not remembered by those official rememberers.

The Early Grades

The whole language movement has had its greatest impact, so far, in the early grades. It is not terribly uncommon to find students writing their own stories, even "books," progressing from invented spellings and elliptic syntax to more standard spellings and syntax over a few years. Indeed, some of these students have done so much reading and writing and "publishing" of their writing that they think of themselves as accomplished authors. In my book *Literacy and Empowerment*, I quoted my six-year-old friend, Nicole Ambrosetti, but when her mother showed her the printed copy of the book and her quotation, she seemed singularly unimpressed. When her mother asked her why she wasn't more excited, she simply said, "I've published lots of things in school, so it's not all that big a deal."

As I hope I made clear in the last chapter, whole language is not a panacea, but the fact is that the teachers I work with find their students much more involved in reading and writing than they used to be. What I am about to suggest, however, goes considerably beyond activities normally associated with the whole language approach. First, it is imperative that teachers encourage (or at the very least avoid *dis*couraging) their students to speak *and write* in their own voices—*becoming increasingly conscious of the characteristics of their primary Discourses*—using the Discourse systems with which they are most comfortable (including free use of their own non-dominant dialects).

Perhaps the most direct way of addressing this is to resurrect the earlier discussion of Sarah Michaels's description of the ways in which Deena and Elliott were treated by their respective teachers. Deena "violated" the teacher's directions because she was not clearly focusing on "one thing." As a result, she was silenced. But in point of fact, the only "mistake" Deena made was to believe that sharing time was real—that she was genuinely being invited to share something that mattered to her, that she was to tell *her* story because *her experience* mattered. Elliott makes a similar mistake: he believes that he is supposed to explain why a particular circus act was important to him by explaining *how it fit into his own experience*. But his teacher knew nothing about his experience, and didn't appear to want to know. Instead of asking about what he had written, she simply told him to delete what she didn't understand. As was discussed in Chapter 3, both students were *wrong* because they made the mistake of attempting to engage in authentic narrative when the teachers' agenda in each case focused on a "kind" of Discourse (school talk/school writing) rather than the content/experience of the speaker/writer. The "rules" of school Discourse preempted the speaker/writer's content *and* Discourse.

What might have been done differently in these two examples? How might the respective teachers have worked with both Deena and Elliott so that they *and* their classmates might have benefitted?

Let's begin with Deena. Sharing time is an important activity and should be treated as such. It's pretty clear that Deena wanted to treat it as such but the teacher was more concerned with assuring that Deena shared her story "correctly." There was no room for Deena's primary Discourse and, therefore, no room for Deena. So first we have to encourage Deena to tell her story her way (it is, after all, hers), and we have to genuinely respect the structure and style she employs in doing so. But because we do not simply want to praise Deena for what she can already do, because we want her to have the opportunity to develop a *metacognitive* sense of her primary Discourse, and because we are teachers, it is our responsibility to do more than patronizingly pat her on the head and say, "Thanks for sharing, Deena."

So what can we do? Well, consider the following scenario, but keep in mind that I am not suggesting that what follows should always be done (a good way to ruin sharing time completely), nor would all of the following activities happen in a single class period. These kinds of activities would be spread out across the school year. Likewise, metacognition, meta-knowledge of any kind does not simply occur because teachers say it should happen as a result of studying something: teachers must structure activities that encourage active reflection on and examination of the language events that become part of the classroom.

As Deena's teacher, I sometimes tape record her (and others') sharing time stories. As a group we use the tapes to write the stories on a blackboard, overhead projector, or on one of the word processors (that generally don't exist in the schools that Deenas go to). The more accurate the transcription of her story, the greater the possibility that we can begin a discussion of the differences between what we do when we "tell" stories as opposed to what we do when we *write* them. Methodologically speaking, such an approach is filled with opportunities: if all of the students have their own taped collections of their stories, they can work individually or collectively trying to "write" their favorite stories. Of course, at the very early grades, such writing will necessarily involve invented spellings, help from the teacher to get words and phrases into print, and so on. And though the going may be slow, students who have chosen their own stories are likely to be engaged in the activity and highly motivated. Again, at early stages, these might be the first "published" works in the classroom as students illustrate and display their stories.

What is being learned here? Quite a bit. For students whose primary Discourse is oral, kids like Deena, who appears to come from a Discourse similar to the one Heath describes in the Tracton community, this kind of activity plays to *their* strengths. Call and response, collective, communal storytelling, playing with language and personal experience—an emphasis on text-based language *growing out of* the interpersonal uses of language that characterize oral Discourses—this approach *includes* the students' Discourses. Likewise, for a boy like Donny, the urban Appalachian discussed in Chapter 3 who has virtually no relation to print nor any understanding what it is for, these early activities introduce him to the concept that oral and printed language are integrally related. Equally important, he learns that his stories matter and that they can be (re)presented in print. Instead of learning that his dialect is inferior and a roadblock to learning, he learns that *his* language, his way of telling, his experience is integral to the school experience. And to the extent that there is any diversity at all in the class, he begins to experience the Discourse systems of others in the class. Given the ability levels of kids at these early stages, they are almost certain to also learn that mistake making, not knowing how to do something, and getting and giving assistance to others in the same boat is constructive activity. For students like Deena and Donny, this represents the beginning stages of learning to read and write.

Keep in mind that as the teacher of this class, I will have many other activities going on throughout the year. I will be reading good stories to the students, engaging them in role-playing activities as a prelude to dramatic activities varying in sophistication as the years go forward. But right now, I want to continue to develop what begins with the "sharing time" activity. Once stories are available on tape and/or written by the students, we can begin to discuss the art of embellishment (or lying), partly because kids can have a lot of fun doing this sort of thing, but even more so because this kind of activity is at the heart of learning how to revise written work. Again, in small or large groups, the students can brainstorm a given story: which elements are the most interesting, how might they be spiced up, what kinds of additions might we add to describe an event or character more fully, which events might we leave out, which need to be elaborated, would it make the story more interesting to rearrange the order of events?

This is the beginning of learning to peer-edit and revise, but it takes place in an imaginative, active way. At this point, again referring to Gee's distinction between *learning* versus *acquiring*, the students are primarily engaged in the process of acquiring. They are not "practicing" revision; they are doing it. In future years, it will be more appropriate to move part of the focus to *learning about* some of these things they will have acquired. But in these early stages, an experiential foundation needs to be poured.

Once the class has engaged in some of the "revising" activities, perhaps even rewriting one another's stories, they can begin the act of critiquing what they have produced. What is the difference between the revised story, the original, and the oral version on the tape? What happens to language and thought as they are moved through these processes? What happens to our experiences as we reshape them through language?

Obviously (I hope), the teacher will shape all of these questions and discussions to fit the developmental level of the kids in the class. But in many ways, these are the same kinds of questions that will be asked over and over, in different forms and with different focuses, as the students move through the school years. Of course, the activities need not be limited to stories that are told during sharing time. Students can orally and in writing begin to create their own versions of the stories I am reading them. Using some of the frameworks presented by Kenneth Koch in *Wishes, Lies, and Dreams*, they can write their own poems and participate in poetry readings.

But a key concept in all these activities is this: all of the activities focus on the students' experiences and primary Discourses, and yet, they are by no means limited to the isolation of either egocentrism or ethnocentrism. Aside from the fact that they are in dialogue with each other, hearing, reading, and revising one another's stories, they are also regularly hearing and viewing stories from the larger culture through the materials that I bring into class to share with them. But even at these early stages, the choice of materials and what we do with them is terribly important. If I want them to experience different Discourse systems, I must bring in representative poetry, stories, songs, and autobiographical pieces written by Native Americans, Asians, African Americans, Puerto Ricans, Mexicans, Anglos. . . . I would read children's fairy tales and fables and myths from various cultural groups and have students "retell" them in terms of their own culture and experience and dialects. What happens if Snow White becomes Sand Brown as she and the dwarfs are Mexican Americans in a predominantly white Texas town? What differences occur if Little Red Riding Hood's journey takes her through a city ghetto instead of a forest? What happens to one of the Coyote stories if it is transported into your school environment? Tell a story about a "trickster" in your neighborhood. The possibilities for these kinds of activities are limitless and present opportunities for students to engage in oral storytelling, writing, and role-playing. But they also allow for the beginning examination of *why* certain changes occur in plot and language as the stories are moved from one environment to another or from one Discourse to another.

At the same time, I would also videotape some of the students' favorite television shows, especially including cartoons. If we are going to help our young people on the road to critical literacy, we absolutely must include helping them to become literate viewers. Bell Hooks speaks powerfully about the importance of watching television *with her family* during her growing up years: "When we sat in our living rooms in the fifties and early sixties watching those few black folks who appeared on television screens, we talked about their performance, but we always talked about the way the white folks were treating them. . . . Watching television in the fifties and sixties, and listening to adult conversation, was one of the primary ways many young black folks learned about race politics." She goes on to say: "Our gaze was not passive. The screen was not a place of escape. It was a place of confrontation and encounter" (1990: 3–4). These comments by hooks are particularly important, not simply because they indicate the potential constructive power of television, but because they clearly emphasize the fact that, for hooks, television viewing was an *active*, communal activity—an activity that was accompanied by critical dialogue. But who would suggest that, for most of our students, television shows provide a "place of confrontation and encounter"? Indeed, the "on" switch for most television sets in our society is an "off" switch for conversation.

But this is not just another diatribe against television viewing. I like to watch television. But I also love to critique and argue about what I watch. Instead of worrying endlessly about kids watching too much TV or the "wrong" kinds of programs, we need to engage them in critical discussions of what they are watching. The *Mighty Morphin Power Rangers*, Mutant Ninja Turtles, and various other cartoons that attract children are often patterned after medieval romances (as with the Star Wars movies): good and evil are often clearly defined and identified; moral action is clear and unambiguous; gender and class roles invite examination. On the one hand, such shows offer the opportunity to examine the melodramatic portrayal of good and evil; on the other hand, even young children need to begin asking how accurately such shows portray the complexity of events in their own lives. Given the enormous influence of television in everyone's lives in this country, it is irresponsible and dangerous to avoid teaching critical media literacy. And we might as well begin in the early grades. But note: this does not mean the teacher can afford to take a patronizing or contemptuous point of view. We are not trying to move the child from low to high culture: the purpose is to help the kids become conscious, critical viewers.

On the other hand, while I am not particularly interested in turning out seven-year-old kids who are good, little "cultural workers," I do believe that some of the particularly innocuous things that often happen in elementary schools might be presented differently in my classroom. Since we have already been discussing the ways in which "stories" change as they are told, retold, and rewritten, the groundwork has been laid for discussions of some of the "stories" that are told about our own and others' histories and how varieties of "embellishment" have been used over the years to change what appears to have actually occurred.

When it is time to celebrate Columbus Day, for example, we might reasonably look at the historical events surrounding the "discovery" of America from the Native American's point of view. At the very least, we might discuss Columbus's use of the word "Indios," the fact that he and his crew enslaved "Indians," and at least begin to introduce our students to the act of counter remembering. At Thanksgiving we might examine the historical events by asking students to write (or tell) the events from the point of view of the Native Americans. Along these lines, it seems to me that the Disney film *Pocahontas* offers an excellent opportunity to engage younger (and older) students in an examination of what happens to (hi)stories when they are transliterated into another medium like a full-length cartoon.

Aside from examining the cartoon itself and the lyrics to the songs in the film, some of which present the overtly racist attitudes of the "invaders," and in addition to examining the concept of female beauty expressed in the caricature of the heroine, the film offers an excellent opportunity for students to find out what historians say about these events and how historical accounts and media representations often differ considerably. Of course, with younger children, we are not talking about a formal research project, but teachers could read condensed historical accounts to the children and make a game of the project: for example, here is what one historian says about these events; who can tell me what parts of the film confirm or contradict what the historian says? The possibilities for using this particular film with younger students seem so obvious to me that I won't go on about it here. But I would also suggest that Disney's *Peter Pan* offers similarly rich classroom possibilities: Why do these children want to avoid growing up? How are females, especially Wendy, portrayed? How are the "Indians" portrayed? What would you do if you had the choice of staying a child? What do you see in the adult world that concerns or worries you?

In addition to using films in this manner, small groups of students could work together to "research" and give class presentations on how other groups celebrate certain holidays and what some of those holidays are: guest speakers might be brought in to talk about Muslim, Jewish, African American, Mexican, Asian holidays and rituals associated with them. Students might write personal narratives explaining how they would feel if they lived in a country that did not celebrate Christmas and Easter and what kinds of letters they would write to school authorities to try to get their own holidays more clearly honored in such schools. This activity might lead to a discussion of how non-Christian students feel in our schools as, year after year, they find themselves surrounded by Christmas carols and creches and Easter stories.

And there would be no hidden agenda involved in any of this—the point is not to bash Christian beliefs or European peoples. The point is to help students begin to be aware of the world in which they live and the different realities created by different Discourse systems. Likewise, the point is not to simply make everything relative and turn it into mush: wrong things have been done throughout history and continue to be done; the holocaust, slavery, the devastation of Native Americans, the invasion of Mexico, the abuse of Chinese labor on the railroads, the mistreatment of Irish. . . . All these things actually occurred and are part of our history.

But again, the objective is not simply negativity nor blind criticism of the dominant culture—the goal is to understand how the dominant culture constructs us and our belief systems. We must remember that these are the early school years, and it would be a terrible mistake to turn the elementary curriculum into nothing more than a debunking of history, just another set of different "facts." I can't think of a better way to turn off young kids than to "politicize" them. And given James Moffett's description of the feelings of the people involved in the West Virginia hostilities, teachers had better be damned careful to remember that the students' primary Discourse is central to their daily existence: any patriarchal or self-righteous dismissal of that fact can accomplish nothing constructive and represents a dismissal of the very people we are trying to teach. Just as Donny's teacher dismissed his mother as "ignorant" because of her dialect, clearly dismissing these Appalachians without knowing anything about them, we need to avoid the "liberal's" patronizing response. To assume that those West Virginia Appalachians are waiting breathlessly to be "liberated" is to guarantee failure. Teachers will have to be conscious of the cultures within which they teach: some groups are likely to be infuriated by the use of television shows in the classroom; others may find the recasting of fairy tales or national heroes to be sacrilegious. In these cases, change must occur carefully and sensitively.

Consequently, what is vitally important in these early stages is that students learn that they can use language, oral and written, to tell *their* stories, to hear/read the stories that others have to tell, and to change the stories. These young people need to gain confidence in and awareness of the fact that *they are literate*, and that their literacy provides them with a powerful ability to act on and interact with those around them. Likewise, they should begin to understand that individuals have been telling stories for many years, and that many of those stories function importantly in what they and others believe is "true." And finally, they should begin, through these early activities, to find some joy in engaging in the process of telling and examining the stories they and others know. It may be only to the extent that teachers welcome and engage the stories of the community that the teachers will find their own "stories" and the stories of other groups admissible.

Middle School Years

In so many schools, the middle school years become one of two things:

1. In well-financed, suburban schools, this becomes a time to worry about whether or not the students have gained/ are gaining "enough" content—are they being prepared to do well on the SAT's, get into the right school, etc. Teachers actually sometimes say to these kids who have reached the ripe old age of 12 that, "It is time to get serious about learning. No more fun and games. It is time for CONTENT, real knowledge. So, when did Columbus discover America and what were the names of the ships?" Time to pull out Hirsch's list? Or,

2. In urban schools, "You kids still don't know how to (read, write, punctuate, paragraph, add, subtract, divide, spell . . .). And we are going to do workbook drills until you have learned to do so" (with careful disregard for the fact that the kids have probably been wasting their time doing such drills for the last six years).

Instead of taking this "adult" perspective about middle schoolers, we would do well to remember that they are still kids, still young, and they have plenty of time to learn all that CONTENT that suddenly seems so important. And please understand that, when I capitalize CONTENT, as I have been, I am not referring to knowledge: I am referring to all the memorization/regurgitation that suddenly comes into prominence around the time middle school begins. Sometimes it seems as though the kids are told to put their imaginations away, forget about their engagement in life and living, dismiss the "childish" things that used to matter, and get down to "business."

I would suggest an entirely different approach. The busyness of business can wait. Among many of the seventh graders I see, video games, MTV, and movie channels have become terribly important. Kids who "have short attention spans" will spend hours playing sophisticated video games and watching television. Others are busy falling in love, dealing with crazed hormone changes, hating their parents, wishing they were someone else. Less lucky ones may also have to try to avoid drive-by shootings, pressures to join gangs, pressure to use and sell drugs. . . . In other words, a lot of stuff is happening to these kids and schools cannot afford to dismiss their lived experiences at this or at any other time.

So what? So they still need to be telling their stories, sharing those stories, and critiquing them. Likewise, the teacher needs to continue introducing them to diverse texts and materials from the broader society, from significant secondary Discourses, to maintain a conscious effort to intrude upon the egocentrism that sometimes seems overwhelming at this period in the students' lives. But they are older: neither children nor adults, they are different, and to simply repeat the same activities from elementary school is to guarantee their boredom.

One immediate problem, however, is that the same kids who used to be so excited about sharing time suddenly become reticent, embarrassed, too "adult" to engage in that stuff. Their private worlds are private; cliques have begun to form in many schools. Whatever innocence was once theirs is quickly giving way to experience. Pipers piping down a valley wild have given way to chimney sweeps; the world is intruding. For many of our students, the world of Blakean innocence is a fiction as they are born into Blake's world of "experience" and the realities of poverty and discrimination.

Holy Thursday

Is this a holy thing to see,
In a rich and fruitful land,
Babes reduced to misery,
Fed with cold and usurous hand?

Is that trembling cry a song?
Can it be a song of joy?
And so many children poor?
It is a land of poverty!

And their sun does never shine,
And their fields are bleak & bare,
And their ways are fill'd with thorns;
It is eternal winter there.

For where-e'er the sun does shine,
And where-e'er the rain does fall:
Babe can never hunger there,
Nor poverty the mind appall.
(William Blake: 19)

And for too many people in our society, too many of our students, it is "eternal winter." Too young to control the intrusive, violent world; too old to hide from it: what's to be done? Well only a fool would begin to suggest a *solution* to quieting the confusion that characterizes this movement from childhood into and through early adolescence. And I certainly offer no solutions. But there are some things that might be done in schools that are different from the kinds of things that make no connections with the students' lives whatsoever. While we are unlikely to be able to offer an eternal summer, we might, at the very least, give our students glimpses of spring.

Almost any medium offers the kind of distance necessary for this age group to tell its stories, especially if teachers are ready to engage the students in active exploration of "point of view" and perspective. Video cameras and tape recorders, for example, offer a wonderful opportunity for students to create their own "movies," news reports, presentations of plays they have written, poetry readings of their own work, their own game shows; tape recorders allow them to conduct "news interviews." Where such materials are not available, and in many poorer areas they are not, we may have to rely on pen and paper, scripted scenarios, and students doing performances. Okay, it's not as good, but it can be done.

However we go about it, it is important to remember that the students probably need and want distance. Although their scripted dramas may be about their own lives (which I would expect), creative writing allows them to distance themselves through the creation of characters and events that do not simply retell a lived experience. As the seeds were sowed in the elementary grades, they now begin to tell their stories through the lenses of other, new perspectives and through whatever media they can get their hands on. They write stories about what happened to the kid who gave himself/herself over to the video game; they write plays about what happens when you try to avoid involvement with gangs or drug pushers. They write about whatever they choose. But more than that, they continue to examine and critique their own productions.

Of course, they have already experimented with some secondary Discourse systems prior to this point, and they continue to use their primary Discourse as they deem fit. But more and more they must be encouraged toward more *conscious* use of a broader range of secondary Discourse systems. Although students in these middle grades may not be particularly conscious of language differences, they have been exposed to them through radio, television, and film. They know that not everyone talks the same way, but it is time for them to work at increasing their consciousness of these differences. Again invoking the distinction between acquiring a Discourse as opposed to studying it, these writers must try to actually *use* different Discourses as they create characters for their stories and plays.

Role-playing activities offer both an effective and interesting way to involve the students in different Discourses. And given their unfamiliarity with some of the Discourse systems and dialects they may wish to use, they are bound to have some difficulties—mistake making is an integral part of learning. Their mistakes, however, need not be occasions for penalty; rather, if we look at all of this as language "play," as young people experimenting with using different styles and dialects to create new realities, making mistakes, identifying and changing inappropriate syntax, etc. should be part of the fun. Also, these kinds of activities go beyond surface structure because the students must also begin to *think about* the ways in which these created characters think.

At this point, however, while I hope it is clear that these are whole language activities because they engage students in a full range of productive language activities (speaking, listening, writing, reading), it may not yet be particularly clear how these activities incorporate the challenge offered by Gardner's theory of multiple intelligences. And a short digression here might help make this clear.

If, as Gardner's research suggests and as I and others believe, the theory of multiple intelligences makes good sense and describes real human beings and their abilities much better than a single score called an Intelligence Quotient, then we need to examine if and how school activities respond to such a theory. First, I think few would disagree that success in school traditionally corresponds to a student's abilities in mathematics and language: readin'-writin'-'n-'rithmetic still rule the day. And even the new educational love affair with computers has done little to change anything. For those of us concerned primarily with literacy, traditional school "language arts" or English activities appear to reward those who come to school with higher degrees of "intelligence" in language-related areas and to ignore (sometimes punish) those whose intelligences are highest in other categories. I think it is more than fair to say that most English classes (most "academic" classes) in our schools do little to recognize those students whose strengths lie in spatial intelligence, musical intelligence, and/or bodily-kinesthetic intelligence (or whatever other categories we may wish to include). And while students with a high degree of "interpersonal intelligence" may do well in our schools, I'm not convinced that we do much to strengthen anyone's "intrapersonal intelligence."

But the reason I raise the issue here, in the middle of a discussion of general classroom methods, is this: it would be relatively simple to accept Gardner's theory, categorize some kids as having high intelligence in a given area, but not, let's say, in language, and throw up our hands in sympathetic understanding and despair. "Oh, poor Jimmy, he lacks linguistic intelligence so there's not much we can do to help him develop his literacy abilities." The point is not to categorize students so we can dismiss them, that's what tracking has been historically about: reward the "gifted" and feel sorry for everyone else. The point here is to develop methods that build off of a student's strengths in order to help the student become stronger in other areas.

Let me illustrate through the following activity. Consider the middle or high school group whose job it is to produce a newscast (or talk show or almost any kind of live television program). Here is a list of things they would need to think about and do:

1. Analyze several major newscasts to find out how they are constructed:
   a. How long is a newscast?
   b. What is the content and where does it come from?
   c. What dialects/Discourse systems does it privilege?
   d. How many and what kinds of advertisements are involved?
   e. What goes on behind the scenes in terms of editing, decisions about what stories are reported in what order, how much time a given story is given, etc.?
2. What kind of set is involved and what equipment is needed to record and present the news?
3. How do reporters "get" the news?
4. What is involved in a news interview or feature story?
5. How does the person in control of the camera control viewer perspective and "shape" a story?
6. To what extent is it possible for the news to be "true": i.e., how does one present an accurate account of an occurrence?
7. How will their particular group go about producing such a complex enterprise:

a. Who will do the "reporting" and news gathering?
b. Who will construct the stage set?
c. Who will make editorial decisions?
d. Who is in charge of advertising?
e. Who is the anchor?
f. Who is in charge of writing the script?
g. How will final decisions be made?

I won't continue this potentially lengthy list; it is intended only as an example. But it should be obvious that in this kind of activity (*as in the real world*) many people work together to produce final products. For example, there is a publishing house for this book, an editor, someone in charge of marketing, readers who helped me make decisions about content and, yes, Discourse. But the school activity I outlined above is not a commercial project, it is a learning activity. Consequently, these student should work together and not in isolation, each employing *and sharing* some area of expertise. The individual who will present the news "on air" may not be a strong writer, but s/he may have good ear for critiquing the language that the writer has used. The person who is technically good with a camera may not have as good a sense of space and perspective as someone else. But because the individual who is not a particularly strong writer works with the writer, making suggestions about how a given report might "sound" better, s/he has the opportunity to begin to *acquire* more facility with the written word. Likewise, the writer who may not be artistically or spatially inclined, by working with the person in charge of the video camera begins to *acquire* greater facility with visual perspective.

By now, I would hope the point is becoming clear. No one activity, not even one as potentially complex and extensive as the "newscast" I've outlined above will *cause* those whose linguistic or spatial intelligence is low to suddenly make great leaps. But over time, over a period of 12 to 16 years (the amount of time we often have students in school), if these kinds of integrated activities become a natural part of the school day, then students are likely to develop across the range of intelligences.

"But," someone might object, "we seem to have left critical pedagogy behind. This may be a neat whole language activity, but it doesn't make students critically aware of how news shows function in the society to make, shape, hide, and manipulate reality." Another legitimate objection might suggest that, while the activity may help students *acquire* greater facility in certain areas, it does not lend itself to helping them gain *meta*-knowledge. And to the extent that the activity ends as I've described it above, both objections would be accurate. Indeed, to the extent any activity is isolated from other activities rather than being perceived as part of a continuum of learning, it is likely that good activities will appear as little more than gimmicky fun things that "we did in Mr. X's class."

Given that there is some question about how much *meta*-anything human beings can achieve before the age of 12 or so, my own inclination is to spend most of the class time in the earlier years keeping students engaged in activities that will help them gain greater facility and literacy within their primary Discourses and in activities that will help them *acquire* a broader range of abilities and Discourses than typify the primary Discourses they bring with them into the school. But beginning around seventh grade and increasing considerably over the high school years, it makes sense to help students begin the process of becoming critically conscious of their own primary Discourses and the Discourses around them. Given that they have been actively experimenting with both primary and secondary Discourses prior to this, the move toward critical examination should be relatively natural. One caution, however: I am by no means suggesting that ninth graders suddenly become adults, especially not from an intellectual or developmental point of view. Too often high schools mark their difference from middle and elementary schools by asserting that: "The fun is over, and now we are going to get down to the real work. So sit still and listen while I give you the information that every American needs to know" (or while I lecture about grammar rules, the meaning of a novel, the importance of the peace treaty at the end of World War I and all the stuff that most kids ignore or forget by lunch time of any given day).

High School

To some extent, the separations I'm using here, especially between high school and middle school are deceiving. The middle school teacher using the news broadcast activity may well include some of what I am going to discuss, but not in quite as much depth. Likewise, the high school teacher should be using activities like the news broadcast, the creative writing activities, etc. that have been suggested for the earlier grades. As I said earlier, both teachers and students need a greater sense of learning and acquisition as part of a continuum, an ongoing, often self-reflective process that moves forward and backward at the same time. One general method for achieving this kind of connective over a student's school years is through the use of student portfolios.

Much of the literature on student portfolios has focused on "assessment of student learning" with the emphasis on collecting student work over time in order for the teachers or system to assess how well a program is working and/or how well students are succeeding in learning whatever "outcomes" have been delineated. But my own greatest interest in something like portfolios is the role they can play in the meta-cognitive growth of the learner.

Too often, for many learners, especially younger learners, school represents a series of isolated, forgettable experiences— even when those experiences may have seemed to be valuable in the moment. Just as Friday often bears little relationship to the previous Monday, for many learners, even more so is September separated from May and sixth grade from ninth. My own position, here, derives from one of the great British poets—William Wordsworth.

[I realize the potential risk I take as I invoke a dead, white male associated with the traditional canon, but I don't think he should be held to task for having been assigned a place in the traditional canon or because he is dead or white. It will be difficult to honor diverse Discourses if we begin by automatically eliminating some of them. In *The End of Education* William Spanos makes a strong argument emphasizing the need to bring non-traditional works onto equal ground with those traditionally associated with the canon, at least in part to avoid destructive binary oppositions (218–219). I interject this point here because some of my suggestions for classroom texts to be used in schools will be misunderstood without it. If we simply take marginalized texts and canonize them, what, really, have we accomplished?]

At first glance, Worsdworth's ideas may seem markedly distant from the world of public schools, non-dominant dialects and non-mainstream dialects. But consider his description of the times in which he lived and their impact on the people: "For a multitude of causes, unknown to former times, are now acting with a combined force to blunt the discriminating powers of the mind, and, unfitting it for all voluntary exertion, to reduce it to a state of almost savage torpor. The most effective of these causes are the great national events which are daily taking place, and the increasing accumulation of men in cities, where the uniformity of their occupations produces a craving for extraordinary incident, which the rapid communication of intelligence hourly gratifies" (*Preface*: 7). At least a little reminiscent of McLaren's description of *Life in the Schools* and the "passion for ignorance" he discusses—right?

It is perhaps one of Wordsworth's greatest (and most ignored) gifts to educators that he so emphasizes the language of the "common man" (and woman) and the importance of self-reflection in moments of tranquility. In one of his most quoted passages, Wordsworth writes that "poetry is the spontaneous overflow of powerful feelings; it takes its origin from emotion recollected in tranquility: the emotion is contemplated till, by a species of reaction, the tranquility gradually disappears, and an emotion, kindred to that which was before the subject of contemplation, is gradually produced, and does itself actually exist in the mind. In this mood successful composition generally begins. . . ." (26). In his poetic vision, the process of self-reflection through writing (poetry) is the central means through which the individual can maintain some kind of consciousness of the ever emerging self and a sense of the changes that occur to that self. Experience is tremendously important: one must go out and do and be. But coming to know experience, gaining an understanding of its importance and meaning depends on quiet, self-reflective thought and language. And while this vision may seem more than a little distant from American high schools and critical pedagogy, I think that is only because so many people "learned about" Wordsworth's poetry without genuinely experiencing it or understanding how it functioned in his world view. Likewise, because of the ways in which schools often distort and ruin great poetry (and so many other things), few students know much of anything about how the French Revolution affected the Romantic poets: how very political many of them were, how deeply committed they were to the promise of a world that genuinely respected the "common man," or how, like Blake or Mary Shelley they were deeply concerned with the effects that "progress" appeared to be having on human beings.

Ah, but I do digress. The point was self-reflection and student portfolios and making connections of experience over time. (So perhaps the above paragraph is not really a digression?)

I would suggest that students, at least as early as sixth grade, regularly write reflective narratives about what they are doing and learning in school. If these seem to be incredibly short and lifeless, it will comment on what is going on (or not going on) in school. But in classrooms as I've described above, where students have been actively engaged in thinking, speaking, listening, reading, writing, performing, viewing, discussing, and critiquing, students are likely to have something to say in these essays. Once a week, such reflective pieces might be written in student journals. Once every four or five weeks, students might review what they've written and write a summary or critical overview of what is they have been doing and learning. These reflective pieces might lead to the students writing self-evaluative pieces at the end of each semester, and these self evaluative pieces might be the entries that would comprise the students' portfolios. By the way, when I mention self-evaluation here, I do not mean that the student is trying to justify a grade or anything like that. Nor do I mean that these would be written entirely without help from the teacher. In this context, self-evaluation represents a reflective examination of "where I've been," joined with a projected articulation of "where I need to go from here."

Especially for the reflective writing that would look back over the semester, students would need to review what they had written in their journals and review the pieces they wrote every four or five weeks. Likewise, students and teacher would benefit from a brainstorming session in which everyone discussed what had happened in the class *and why* it had happened (or what had not happened and should have happened). The written self-evaluations might best focus on students trying to discuss which class activities had been most rewarding and why; which they learned the least from and why; which they wish they had worked at more diligently. And while this is distinctly not a book on student assessment, nor are portfolios a novel idea, I would suggest that this kind of writing collected over time would make "report cards" look as silly as many of us know they are.

But back to the role these reflective writings and portfolios might play over time in our schools, especially as they might lead to higher degrees of metacognition for our students. If the students doing the "news broadcast activity" in eighth grade had written reflectively about it, they could refer to these pieces of writing in tenth grade when they participated in a similar activity, perhaps one in which they viewed and compared several different news broadcasts recorded on the same evening covering the same set of events with the ways in which a major newspaper covered the events. Thinking back to that earlier time when they produced a news show, they might begin to reconsider the power of the press in our society and the differences between print news and broadcast news. They might rewrite some of the stories themselves using a different slant to "shape" reality. Again, given the central role played by television in our society, I would think it particularly important to continue having students view and critique various shows and advertising on television varying from talk shows to MTV to CNN to sit-coms to soaps.

But portfolios like the ones I mentioned might also serve in important ways to include students in their learning processes. Students entering high school English classes (or any class, for that matter) might review what they had written about over the middle school years and come up with suggestions for some of the kinds of things that *they* think they ought to be doing in the coming year. As they review earlier portfolio entries, they might discover/remember issues that, from this somewhat more mature perspective, they want to pursue further. Of course, in many urban schools the student population changes rather rapidly as families move in and out of the community for various reasons. Under these conditions, some students might have no portfolios to reflect on. But while this causes some problems, these students should still be encouraged into doing some reflective writing, perhaps trying to write about what they remember learning in earlier grades at other schools. At the very least, this may engage them in the new class and it should give the teacher a window on their past experience.

The Place of Literature

So far I've said relatively little about literature, and I would like to move toward the a discussion of some of the ways that literature might play an important and interesting role in a whole language approach to teaching literacy that also emphasizes critical, liberatory thinking.

June Jordan tells the story about having her college students translate passages from Alice Walker's *The Color Purple* into standard English. Of course, the activity was entirely new for these students who had never seen their primary Discourse/ dialect in print, and everyone had a good time laughing at what happens to Celie's voice and content as it is converted into standard English. But activities like this are more than gimmicks to give everyone a good laugh, as Jordan clearly knew. When students are given the opportunity to work with language in these ways, they begin to see that different Discourses and dialects communicate in different ways and that being able to employ different Discourses and dialects gives writers (including the students) more possibilities for making a point powerfully and clearly.

I've tried a similar activity with students in an adolescent literature class using the novel *The Adventures of Huckleberry Finn* by Mark Twain. I like using the novel because it raises so many issues that often remain unexamined in many classrooms, at the same time I know that my own stress level goes up every time I teach it. I have had both black and white students become understandably upset by the use of the word "nigger." I had a black student explain, sincerely and in standard dialect, that Jim's dialect indicated he was inherently stupid, occasioning a careful look at Jim's intelligence or lack thereof. And I've watched students become increasingly understanding of Jim's intelligence, sensitivity, and total entrapment.

In my experience, some white students and some African American students—almost anyone whose primary Discourse is essentially in standard English—have difficulty understanding Jim's dialect. Many students have trouble reading the novel at all until they give up on their attempts to phonically reproduce Jim's dialogue (even college students remain disabled by phonics instructions, sometimes). Normally their reading problems begin to disappear after I read some sections using both Jim's and Huck's dialects and convince the students that they have to read for meaning rather than trying to sound out the words. But the fun begins when they try to translate sections of the novel into standard English.

I have them do this in pairs, each pair working on a different section of the novel, and the results are fascinating. After each pair has worked for 20 minutes or so, we come back together as a group and examine the results. First, one student in the pair tries to read the original dialect, usually finding it pretty difficult. Next they read the standard English version, and as in Jordan's experience, everyone gets a good laugh because the "voices" of the novel are entirely lost and the content becomes comic because it is so distorted by the standard English version. One fascinating thing I've seen occur in this activity is that students have difficulty moving some parts into standard dialect because the non-dominant regional dialect is "the only way to say it."[1]

Because the novel is told entirely through Huck's perspective, a fact many younger readers miss entirely, at first, the reader's perspective is controlled and limited. But also because of this fact, readers can, and I think should, rewrite parts of the novel from Jim's perspective. And this activity involves considerably more than moving from one dialect to another.

Indeed, I think this may be one of the most important ways to help readers understand the reasons that the novel receives so much critical attention. Once one rethinks ("rewrites") some of the incidents from Jim's point of view, Jim's entrapment and victimization become clearer than ever. Here is an intelligent man, trying to escape to freedom, who must follow the whims of an adolescent. Subjected to Huck's foolishness, Jim misses his one chance for escape, floating past Cairo in the fog, and is now destined to follow the river even further south. And it is only as one takes Jim's perspective that the underly-

1. Special thanks to Johnna Conti and Michelle Marsh, two of our Learning Center Tutors who introduced me and others to this activity during a tutoring workshop.

ing terror of the novel becomes clear: his freedom and his life
always at risk, he must do whatever the Duke and King make
him do and be subjected to the demeaning and dangerous
games that Tom and Huck play with Jim's life at the end of the
novel. I don't begin to know Twain's intent, but examined from
the perspective I suggest above, the novel becomes a metaphorical description of how African slaves were treated—less
powerful than an outcast adolescent, the playthings of an entire society, entirely dehumanized, victims of torture.

Having students explore literature from different points of
view can be an important and powerful activity in may cases,
just as having them play around with different Discourses and
dialects is also revealing. Hawthorne's *The Scarlet Letter* offers
one more example, and I choose it because it is one of those
novels so carefully ruined for so many readers because of the
ways in which it is often taught. Like Golding's *Lord of the Flies*,
The Scarlet Letter sometimes seems to have been condemned to
being used to show students how *symbols* "work" in literature.
Students find out, quickly, that the rose at the beginning of
the novel is a symbol. The scarlet *A*, of course, is a symbol.
The forest is a symbol, and the town is a symbol. Pearl is a
symbol. The stars in the sky are symbols. Indeed, everything is
a symbol. One would think that Hawthorne sat down with the
intention of writing something with lots of symbols so teachers could use it to teach symbols. Sadly, in the midst of all
these symbols, the novel gets lost. When literature is taught in
this manner, students have no reason to read it at all; by their
own admission, they simply (and sensibly) wait for the teacher
to tell them whatever it is they must remember for a test (theme,
symbols, etc.).

But Hawthorne's novel is a complex, troubling depiction of
the place and treatment of women in a patriarchal "new" world.
Hawthorne offers an incredibly powerful female protagonist
in Hester Prynne at the same time that he powerfully depicts
the victimization of women, the destructive self-righteousness
of a community, human hypocrisy and viciousness, and the
promise of feminism. As with Twain, or any author for that
matter, I do not pretend to know Hawthorne's intent, but I do
know that when students begin to rethink the novel from
Hester's point of view and to think from within Pearl instead

of always being controlled by the narrator's point of view, the novel begins to change for them. And from a liberatory viewpoint, these kinds of activities can work importantly for students to reconsider the ways in which their own society is constructed, the ways in which similar hypocrisies evidence themselves.

Also, as with Twain's novel, this novel offers students an opportunity to move beyond the study of literature *as* literature and begin to examine historical issues that serve importantly in the process or remembrance and the invoking of counter-memory. Behind and underneath this novel, barely surfacing, is the historical foundation for the oppression of women that continues to function in our own and many other societies, not to mention the stereotyping of Native Americans. Students have a right to examine and should examine the ideas of the Puritans, especially *as they have continued to function in our society.* The witch trials conducted by males to steal property from women and "keep women in their place," the continuation of the Adam and Eve syndrome in which the wicked woman causes the downfall of the righteous man, a religion that terrorizes its believers: it wasn't all just about the first Thanksgiving!

Likewise, when they work with the language of this novel—dense, descriptive language—and begin to rework it in terms of dialect, everything begins to change. This is particularly interesting when students "modernize" the novel, moving it into a modern urban setting, examining the plight of women and people who do not fit the societal dictates and mores. Hester, after all, is an unwed mother: how does society treat her and her child? How does this compare with the ways in which we treat single mothers? Why do we look down upon these people? For those willing to work with a powerful juxtaposition, students might relate their study of *The Scarlet Letter* to a study of James Baldwin's *If Beale Street Could Talk*—a novel in which Baldwin presents a very different look a how some young African Americans deal with pregnancy out of wedlock and mistreatment by dominant authorities.

But my point here is not to argue for specific works of literature. There is such an abundance of good literature written across time and across cultures that one wonders how anyone could possibly support the concept of a limited and limiting canon. And literature being what it is, the kinds of activities I've been discussing can be used with many works. My point, rather, is that any single critical approach that governs the teaching of literary works (or anything else for that matter) is both limited and limiting. Feminist, neo-Marxist, personal response, historical—the teacher must be prepared to help students work with the text in a variety of ways so that it functions as a living part of the storytelling and sharing of stories that began in elementary grades.

But the same is true for the "literature" of the electronic media, as I suggested earlier. Certainly many teachers have used novels that were used as the basis for films, though often the experience seems to involve little more than viewing the film, and treating it as something that exists so that students can be tested on its contents. It is not a particularly new observation to suggest that many teachers are far more at home with printed texts than they are with film and audio, but if we are going to help students live critically and consciously in this world, we cannot let our own limitations construct curricula.

In terms of different dialects and Discourses, one particularly inviting pairing is Carolyn Chute's *The Beans of Egypt Maine* and the related film, *Forbidden Choices* (directed by Jennifer Warren). Chute presents us with a backwoods clan of ill-educated, poverty stricken people whose lives involve rape, child and wife beating, starvation, incest, humor, love, hardship, rage, entrapment. . . . It is a powerfully written, tough novel. I emphasize it in this discussion because the students' responses to it are complex and unusual. As I mentioned earlier, I sometimes teach a course in adolescent literature with a focus on multicultural literatures. I use novels about the Black experience (Paule Marshall, Toni Morrison), one about a Pakistani female (*Shabanu* by Susanne Fisher Staples), Sandra Cisneros's work, the writings of James Welch and Leslie Silko and other Native Americans—a broad range of literature crossing several different cultures. The point of the course is to introduce students to the works as works of art *and* to engage them in discussions of difference. Always they are reminded that a single novel presents a single set of experiences; it does not present an entire culture, nor even necessarily a large segment of a culture. So none of us is trying to say, "Here, read this and you'll know about Pakistanis, or Jews, or Africans. . . ."

At any rate, what I find fascinating is this: students are able to (appear to) deal rationally and sensitively with most of the events and characters in the literary works, but when we get to the Beans and their life style, everything changes. And by and large, this generalization about student responses is true for middle and lower-middle class students, white students and minority students alike. Students who can achieve some distance in a discussion of Toni Morrison's *The Bluest Eye* or the characters who populate Cisneros's *House on Mango St.* just can't tolerate the Beans. And while I'm not sure why this occurs, I suspect it has something to do with the fact that none of the students, regardless of background, is accustomed to thinking about *white* folks who live as the Beans do. Some students are so alienated by the backwoods world of the Beans that they find it difficult to think of them as human beings. Of course, my point is not that we should simply search for shocking works to teach, but that we should look for works that directly challenge the comfortable accommodations that many students have made as they "accept" people from other cultures.

Likewise, in this particular case, the film offers an opportunity to examine how print is transformed into film, how the director and actors interpret and create the characters and experiences, and in what ways the film constructs the viewer and the society. Also, at any point in working with either the novel or the film, students can discuss what would happen if the dialects were standard English: what would this do to the reader/viewer's experience; how would it change the impact of the works; and why? As I've already said, if we are going to emphasize critical literacy, we must be much more open to the examination of the texts that are presented in the electronic media. And this agenda must go well beyond the use of films. Like it or not, children and adults alike spend enormous amounts of time watching television: to what extent are they critical viewers? To what extent have schools helped them to be literate viewers or listeners. MTV's popularity and influence (conceptual and economic) is far reaching and powerful. Instead of making uninformed comments about the music and accompanying videos, teachers must engage students in a critical examination of such a medium. We need to be more alert and open to seeing that the Puritan treatment of women and the representation of women in some of those music videos is closely related. Students need to consider the economics of the music business and ask how *they are constructed* by these powerful media.

At the same time, it is much too easy to take a simplistic point of view toward the music that our students listen to. For many of our students, song lyrics represent the only poetry with which they are familiar, and for some the lyrics are powerfully meaningful. Having earlier asserted that I believe we need to teach works by some of the dead, white males who represent the canon, I now take the risk of offending another set of readers. I enjoy listening to Nirvana and Pearl Jam and Blues Traveler, Garland Jeffries, Buckwheat Zydeco, and Ladysmith Black Mambazo. But I'm not simply talking about "enjoyment" here: Bob Dylan, Neil Young, many rappers, Tracy Chapman, Bob Marley, Robbie Robertson and a host of other popular musicians and song writers produce music and lyrics tied directly to the lives of us and our students. Life in the streets, life in the ghetto, drive-by shootings, drug abuse, political commentary, the "ethnic cleansing" of Native Americans, the pain and joy of daily living—these are the topics of this living poetry.

Of course, the artists I've mentioned above are some of *my* choices, and I would use some of their works because students need to be introduced to more of everything than their private worlds include. For the music they are most immediately engaged in, all one needs to do in most schools is ask the students to identify some of the songs that they find particularly important, have them bring them into class, and make them the focal point of critical discussion. But let me be very clear about what I do and do not mean by "critical discussion": first and foremost, I am not suggesting that teachers dissect these lyrics in terms of rhyme scheme, metrics, and so on. While there may be a place for such a discussion at some point, it is generally a good way to ruin the entire experience for the students. I am absolutely convinced that we can ruin Joan Osbourne or Cassandra Wilson as effectively as we've ruined

Wordsworth and Dickinson. So by critical discussion, I mean that students need to engage the meaning of the lyrics, the choices of images that the writer uses and the feelings/thoughts they invoke. They need to discuss the extent to which the lyrics describe realities in their own lives. They need to *think* about this stuff instead of simply "being there" with the rhythm as the song passes into the air. But one last point about the use of electronic media and popular culture in the classroom: don't expect miracles. Just because it is contemporary does not automatically mean that it will break through that "passion for ignorance." Many students have learned to expect very little in the classroom, and older students in particular have become all too accustomed to tuning out school events, no matter how hip the classroom activity may appear to be.

Of course, it is probably clear at this point that much that I've discussed as appropriate for the "high school level" is equally appropriate for the college level. But let's formalize it anyway.

College

One of the reasons that I incorporated some of the activities I use in my college classes under the "High School" heading is that many of the students who most deserve an opportunity to get involved in interesting approaches to language and literacy, dialects and Discourse systems, and the aims of critical pedagogy are students who never make it to college. It may be that some small percentage of them never make it to college because they are not very bright, but as we all know, many do not make it because they can't afford it or because their dialect/Discourse systems are discriminated against on standardized tests guaranteed to keep them out of higher education. It is my hope that, if more activities like the ones discussed above were used in the public schools, more of these students would gain the necessary awareness to do one or both of the following: (1) learn to use the system and make it work for them; and/or (2) fight and eliminate the elements that systematically exclude them from success in higher education.

On the other hand, if those who teach in the nation's colleges and universities do not do something to improve the ways these students are taught and the ways in which their "different" dialects and Discourse systems are treated, it may not matter if they get to college. Sensing doom, they will revert to the kinds of destructive resistance and that passion for ignorance that McLaren describes. (As I reread that last sentence, I realize that it suggests that everyone who stays in college has a passion for knowledge: I would simply suggest that the passion for ignorance can be reflected in the *B* student who has simply learned how to do well on multiple choice tests and jive the teacher during office hours. There are plenty of college graduates whose passion for ignorance is both stunning and observable, just as there are plenty of people who never went to college whose passion for knowing is equally stunning.)

But this is about classroom methods. I have found my own students absolutely fascinated with discussions of dialect and Discourse, and I firmly believe that this might be one of the central foci of freshman English courses. And if any course in higher education needs to be interrogated, it is the freshmen English course that is required of so many students in so many colleges and universities. By and large, freshmen English is viewed as a course that is supposed to "fix" all the writing problems that these "careless" young people never bothered to learn in earlier years. And with all the wonderful research and work that has been done on suggesting new practices for freshmen English courses, they have proved incredibly resistant to change. With all due respect, I think this occurs, in part, because most Ph.D.'s in English know almost nothing about teaching in general and less about teaching writing. In fact, Ph.D.'s in general know almost nothing about teaching in their various disciplines: why would they? Most graduate programs are so esoteric and research/content oriented that issues having to do with teaching, especially teaching undergraduates, are seldom discussed. Those who do become good teachers, and there are many, do so through their own intuitions and because they bother to seek help from more experienced colleagues. Some even listen to their students. Little wonder then that general education programs are relatively abysmal across higher education; and less wonder that changes such as those advocated in this book and, especially this chapter, will find it slow going in higher education.

Of course, many universities "train" their teaching assistants to some degree, often emphasizing the "process" approach in one way or another. And some do an exceptionally fine job of helping these teaching assistants become good writing teachers. But the fact is that such "training" too often lasts a relatively short period of time and resorts to an emphasis on the use of specific methods as part of a lockstep curriculum tied to a specific composition text. The result is that the teaching assistants, having been given relatively little help, resort to teaching a fairly standard rhetorical approach to teaching writing. The simple fact is that people who teach the composing process need to have more than a smattering of knowledge about language, learning theory, and discourse theory if they are to teach writing effectively—and especially if they are to teach writing to students whose dialect/Discourse is non-dominant. Of course, they are unlikely to gain such knowledge if the people "training" them do not have it.

But the point here is much more than a simple, reductivist criticism of teaching in colleges and universities. My point is that the kinds of activities I've been discussing and the theoretical and philosophical discussion prior to this chapter that lead to this discussion of methods have implications for teaching far beyond English and the language arts in general. Sociology, political "science," economics, philosophy, history, education, foreign languages, art, music, mathematics, the sciences, business—you make the list: Which of these areas should not focus on student experiences? Which of these areas can legitimately claim to teach students and, at the same time, dismiss a theory of multiple intelligences? Of course, the answer is simple: as long as any of these disciplines see themselves to be defined entirely in terms of bodies of content—discrete skills and fragmented areas of knowledge—they can easily afford to dismiss just about everything in this book. But of what use is a body of knowledge for the individual who cannot think critically about a discipline and question the ways in which the discipline constructs both the notion of knowledge and the "knowers" who are in the discipline? Likewise, of what use is a body of knowledge that is separate from all other bodies of knowledge? Of course, the challenges inherent in these remarks are not solely directed at college teachers, but colleges prepare the teachers who teach in elementary, middle, and high schools. And those teachers are not very likely to undergo a radical turnaround without some leadership and help. On the other hand, in fairness to teachers of grades K–12, one is far more likely to find student-centered teachers in these grades than in university settings.

One problem that has to be addressed immediately is this: standard English and academic or essayist literacy are more entrenched in higher education than they are at any other point on the educational continuum. One can enter almost any discussion among faculty in almost any discipline and hear about the sorry state of student literacy. And while I think that there is a serious problem with student literacy, including the literacy of college graduates, I do not think it is a matter of expertise in standard English or essayist literacy. Rather, it is related to that "passion for ignorance": why would we expect students who have been taught that learning has something to do with memorizing fragmented, discrete bits of information in order to pass multiple choice tests to have a deep hunger for knowing?

Consequently, if anything is to change, college and university teachers must reconsider the value of a course taught primarily through lectures to large (or small) groups of students who are busily taking notes or sleeping. One of my concerns about teaching the tenets of critical pedagogy to education students at the college level is that the college professor's missionary zeal may lead to the same kinds of teaching that always characterized higher education: teacher as deliverer of knowledge; student as passive receiver. As I write this, I think of the education classes I've seen in which the "liberal" professor *lectures* about the importance of small-group work, classroom discussion, and focusing on the needs, experiences, and voices of individual students. If the discussion of *acquisition versus learning* is to mean anything, it means that college teachers must involve students in activities that create the possibility for acquisition of new Discourses *and* for activities that encourage *learning about* (meta-knowledge) that which is being acquired. I remind all of us that the opening quote from Aronowitz and Giroux asserts the need for students to author their own voices—an emphasis that I believe is absolutely es-

sential to learning. But Aronowitz and Giroux also assert the
need for *affirmation and interrogation* of the experiences the
students voice.

For decades, perhaps forever, higher education has focused
on *learning*, giving students information *about* disciplines.
While the intentions have probably been good, the results have
been students who know very little about much outside of their
immediate majors. On the other hand, a perceived and at times
real danger of student-centered teaching and a limited notion
of the essentials of the whole language approach may accomplish just the opposite: so much attention given to the students'
experiences and affirmation of them that students learn little
of anything other than to feel good about their "voices." But a
marriage of the two extremes makes good sense: activities encouraging acquisition first, followed by and sometimes simultaneously joined with activities that interrogate that which is
being (or has been) acquired.

This also means that teachers in higher education must see
that their oft cited notions about equality across gender, race,
and class must be joined with an acceptance and understanding of the validity of dialects and Discourses that are different
from that of the dominant culture. And given the depth of
ignorance and bias in the academy toward non-dominant dialects and Discourses, this is going to take some real work on
the part of the academy at large—work that goes far beyond
individual classrooms. What follows and ends this discussion
is a list of changes that *faculty* must cause to occur; to wait for
administrators to do this work is to escape responsibility and
guarantee that victimization will continue.

1. End the use of SAT's and ACT's as part of the applica-
    tion/admission procedure.
2. Eliminate "placement" essays imposed on students at
    orientation sessions and used to place them in "reme-
    dial" composition courses.
3. Encourage the use of portfolios of student work as part
    of the admission procedure.
4. Change freshmen English courses so that they accept
    difference in dialect and Discourse without patroniza-
    tion or discrimination.

5. Engage students in all courses in the examination of and experimentation with various dialects and Discourse systems.
6. Increase reflective thinking/writing activities in all disciplines.
7. Re-examine general education programs by asking to what extent they engage the students' experiences and encourage students to be critically literate *across* disciplines.
8. Examine Departmental and Program curricula by asking whether or not they focus primarily on discrete areas of knowledge or engage students in the processes of acquisition and learning.
9. Eliminate multiple-choice tests, or, at the very least, insure that other means of assessment are used that allow students to have a real voice in the process, explaining what they know, rather than simply asking them to identify what someone has decided they should know.
10. Open up the canon (every discipline has one): note I did not suggest eliminating the canon; simply explode it by making it inclusionary rather than exclusionary.

I'll stop there. Any implementation of these ten points would offer a wonderful opportunity to change the Discourse of higher education in particular and education in general. Really, all this is about is letting the students in as *participants* in the critical educational enterprise. What a thought! On the other hand, given the powerful forces at large in society who wish to reduce funding to education at all levels, see larger class sizes, create "more efficient" teaching (delivery systems), more "assessment" (testing), and higher "standards," what I am suggesting is going to be difficult to achieve, arduous, and tension filled.

On the other hand, let's do it before it do us (any more than it already has).

Chapter 6

Postscript: Discourse in Cyberspace

Most of the previous discussion has focused on Discourse differences most markedly associated with ethnicity, race, class, and gender. As a result, one particularly important secondary Discourse has remained unaddressed: the Discourse of cyberspace or the world wide web. It may be that what Michael Specter, writing for the *New York Times*, suggests is true: "Perhaps only the car, the pill and television have had a more immediate impact on the habits of 20th century Americans" (1).

While I believe it is much too soon to present clear descriptions of this new phenomenon, especially to suggest that it represents a single Discourse, I also believe that the issue must be briefly addressed. Anyone familiar with e-mail, listserves, MOOS, "the web," and so on knows that considerable discussion is focusing both on the educational uses and possibilities inherent in this new technology and on the effects such technology may have on the nature of written communication. The issues become particularly important when we consider the possibility of very young children who, instead of having their initial "literacy" experiences comprised of parents reading books to them and the experiments they conduct with crayons and living room walls, suddenly find themselves "playing" with computer programs. Of course, I don't mean to suggest that children's books will disappear or that children will no longer scribble their ways to print literacy. But the fact is that we may be looking toward a future in which the use of networked computers, in both homes and schools, connected to the world wide web will shape the initial and sequentially more sophisticated literacy experiences of our young.

What follows is a brief list of the frequently asked questions (FAQ) and issues that surround this new Discourse and the effects it may have on the very nature of written communication.

1. Most of us associate narrative and exposition with fully developed discussion/explanation of a given topic (whether that development is shaped by call and response or traditional rules of essayist literacy or whatever). But most e-mail messages tend to be relatively brief. And even more obviously, the kinds of things we see on most listserves tend to be brief, seldom fully developed, and "pieces" of an ongoing dialogue which suggests something like an infinitely growing thread of commentary conducted among a group of authors rather than a set piece written by a single author. Indeed, it is common for those participating on listserves to apologize if their statements get too long, worrying, perhaps, about shows of egotism (?) and/or overtaxing someone else's electronic "mailbox."

2. Anyone who has been involved with "chat rooms" or programs that allow for relatively unmediated, ongoing written dialogue has experienced a new kind of Discourse. In this arena it is not unusual to find individuals who know almost nothing about one another discussing a topic about which the participants may or may not have any genuine information, and in relatively fragmented utterances. Again, the shape of the written discourse is often one that grows almost organically and often moves far away from whatever was the beginning focal point.

3. Those who have read many web pages or articles written for electronic magazines (zines) are familiar with how radically such a "literacy experience" contrasts with the experience of reading normal print. Instead of beginning at page one and moving sequentially through a text, in cyberspace the reader is often invited to construct his/her own organization of the text, jumping from one embedded link to another in what can be a relatively haphazard manner. Indeed, it is common to find oneself invited to jump from one article or web page to another article or web page, in what, sometimes, feels like an infinite

progression toward a relatively unknown end and through almost completely uncharted (cyber)space. I am sure that some readers identify with the experience of having been surfing the web for several hours only to realize that, in addition to experiencing eye fatigue, they have also experienced cognitive dissonance and are not at all sure where exactly it is they have "been" for those several hours.

4. Of course, many homes and schools are still without networked computers, but numbers are growing daily and many teachers already have their students, even in elementary grades, experimenting with interactive writing programs, the web, the creation of web pages, listserves, and e-mail. Some universities and colleges are moving toward writing courses that are entirely computer based and replace what was formerly known as "freshmen composition." And the questions about how this will shape these students' notions of "print literacy" abound. Perhaps even more interesting, however, is the question suggested in #3 above: how will these experiences shape the cognitive processes of these learners?

These four points barely scratch the surface of the questions and issues that surround the explosion of computer-based communication through world wide networks. Some may envision a Derridean world of language anarchically spiraling further and further away from the writer, a world in which meaning is never "located" but always being supplemented and further dissociated by "other" subjects. Others may envision a democratizing of literacy, a new world in which meaning making is always the result of collaborative processes, a world in which the dominant authorities and standard bearers lose almost all control of the world of literacy. Some find all of this threatening; others find it empowering.

At present, I find it not at all threatening, nor am I at all sure just where all this is going to go. The fact is that young and old alike are populating cyberspace and many are thriving in it. And as is generally the case with changes in language and Discourse, these changes are likely to develop regardless of whether we approve or disapprove. As has been my point throughout much of this book, however, I believe it is most important for all of us to be conscious of the existence of this new Discourse arena and of the ways in which it differs from the nature of literacy as we have known it. Will we less and less communicate and teach f2f (face to face)? IMHO (in my humble opinion), f2f teaching will not disappear because humans will remain in need of human contact and interaction. But for those of us who believe that literacy is important, it is essential that we attempt to improve our own literacy in this dynamic, new area. Since netoric is here, we might as well begin our own attempts at fluency. Besides that, once you get beyond technophobia, it's really kind of fun, just like most reading and writing.

If the kinds of technology I've been discussing are made easily accessible to *all* students, it is conceivable that our students' interactions in cyberspace will have greater impact on the nature of literacy than any given event in the last several decades. These technologies—computers, on-line networks, and the web all offer students much broader opportunities to experiment in writing with their own primary Discourses *and to interact* with real audiences and a rich variety of other, secondary Discourses. As I write this I am thinking of a listserve I subscribed to that focused on multicultural education. It was not at all unusual on this particular list to read messages that were written by people for whom English was a second language and by people whose dialect was distinctly non-dominant. Not surprisingly, these language differences caused no one any problems that I could discern.

On the other hand, if economic privilege continues to function in schools as it has been, then it is relatively clear that students in financially strapped schools (i.e., most inner-city schools and many rural schools) will find themselves at even greater disadvantages than those they presently experience. In short, this new technology can either be used to enrich the development of literacies among all our students, or it can be used to create even greater distance between the dominant haves and the non-dominant have-nots.

For those who are new to the experience and are interested in sampling some of the discussions surrounding these issues as they are represented on the web, I offer this highly selective list.

A. *Kairos* is a scholarly magazine located at
    http://english.ttu.edu/kairos/1.2/tocnf.html

This magazine is edited by Mick Doherty and prints html articles, reviews, and discussions focusing on theory and practice associated with the use of networked computers in the teaching of writing in webbed environments.

B. A good beginning point for those who want to join a listserve is the Alliance for Computer and Writing—ACW at
    acw-listserv.ttu.edu

Participants on this list range from newbies to people who have been long involved in using networked computers in their classrooms. The discussions are very helpful and the participants more than willing to help beginners.

C. Computer-Mediated Communication Studies Center at
    http://www.december.com/cmc/study/center/html

Among other things, this address will provide access to *CMC Magazine*, a journal containing articles of interest to almost anyone interested in theory and practice associated with the use of computers on educational settings.

D. Selfe, Cynthia, and Susan Hilligloss, eds. *Literacy and Computers: The Complications of Teaching and Learning with Technology*. New York, NY: Modern Language Association of America, 1994.

This is a very helpful collection of essays exploring a broad range of important issues connected with literacy and classsroom applications of computer technology. It offers a good beginning point for those who are new to technology/classroom issues.

E. Kling, Rob. *Computerization and Controversy: Value Conflicts and Social Choices*. San Diego, CA: Academic Press, 1996.

This book offers an interesting beginning point for readers who want to survey some of the major issues surrounding the use of computers and communication.

This is admittedly a very short list of sources, but the reasons are probably apparent to anyone who already uses the web and listserves. Listserves come and go with blinding speed, and the ones I've listed above may not exist by the time a reader of this book tries to access them. Quite simply, the best way to learn about much that has been written in this brief postscript is to get yourself networked and start surfing the web for sources of information. In terms of books written about computers and social-educational issues, choices abound as any library search will indicate. Consequently, the above list is intended more as an example of what is available than a selective recommendation.

Good luck. :-)

Bibliography

Amiran, Minda Rae, and Patrick L. Courts. "The Evolution of a System of Portfolio Assessment in the English Department." *Faculty Perspectives: Sharing Ideas on Assessment.* Ed. James R. Chen. Albany, NY: University Faculty Senate, 1994: 14-18. Paper delivered at Conference on Assessment in English and Mathematics, October 1993, sponsored by State University of New York Faculty Senate.

Anderson, Gary L., and Patricia Irvine. "Informing Critical Literacy with Ethnography." In Lankshear and McLaren: 81-104.

Anzaldúa, Gloria. *Borderlands: La Frontera.* San Francisco: Spinsters/Aunt Lute, 1987.

Apple, Michael W. "Between Moral Regulation and Democracy: The Cultural Contradictions of the Text." In Lankshear and McLaren: 193-216.

Aronowitz, Stanley, and Henry A. Giroux. *Postmodern Education.* Minneapolis: University of Minnesota Press, 1991.

Ashton-Jones, Evelyn. "Feminist Critique of Collaborative Learning." Unpublished manuscript, 1992.

Atwell, Nancy. *In the Middle: Writing, Reading, and Learning with Adolescents.* Portsmouth, NH: Boynton/Cook, 1987.

Ball, Arnetha F. "Expository Writing Patterns of African American Students." *English Journal* (January 1996): 27-35.

Bee, Barbara. "Critical Literacy and the Politics of Gender." In Lankshear and McLaren: 105-132.

Blake, William. "Holy Thursday." *The Poetry and Prose of William Blake*. Ed. David V. Erdman with commentary by Harold Bloom. Garden City, NY: Doubleday and Company, Inc., 1970.

Blanton, Linda L. "Southern Appalachia: Social Considerations of Speech," Ch. IV in J. L. Dillard, *Toward a Social History of American English*. New York: Mouton, 1985: 73–90.

Bloom, Alan. *The Closing of the American Mind: How Higher Education Has Failed Democracy and Impoverished the Souls of Today's Students*. New York: Simon and Schuster, 1987.

Bloom, Paul. "Overview: Controversies in Language Acquisition." In P. Bloom: 5–48.

———, ed. *Language Acquisition*. Cambridge, MA: The MIT Press, 1994.

Britton, James. *Language and Learning*. Coral Gables, FL: University of Miami Press, 1970.

Broder, David S. "Dole Supports English as the U.S. Language." From the *Washington Post* printed in *The Buffalo News* (September 9, 1995): A–1, 8.

Brown, Joseph Epes. "Becoming Part of It." In Dooling and Jordan-Smith: 9–20.

Buckley, Thomas. "Doing Your Own Thinking." In Dooling and Jordan-Smith: 36–52.

Cai, Guanjun. "Beyond 'Bad Writing': Teaching English Composition to Chinese Students." Paper delivered at College Composition and Communication Conference, San Diego, March 31–April 3, 1993.

Chambers, K., and P. Trudgill. *Dialectlogy*. Cambridge, England: Cambridge University Press, 1980.

Chomsky, Noam. *Language and Politics*. Ed. C. P. Otero. New York: Black and Rose Books, 1988.

Coates, Jennifer. "Introduction." In Coates and Cameron: 64–73.

Coates, Jennifer, and Deborah Cameron, eds. *Women in Their Speech Communities: New Perspective on Language and Sex.* London: Longman, 1988.

Collins, James. "Some Problems and Purposes of Narrative Analysis in Educational Research." *Journal of Education* 167:1 (1985): 57–70.

Conference on College Composition and Communication. 1974. "Students' Right to Their Own Language." *College Composition and Communication* 25.3 (Fall): 1–32.

Conklin, Nancy Faires, and Margaret A. Lourie. *A Host of Tongues: Language Communities in the United States.* New York: The Press, 1983.

Council Chronicle. "Former NEH Chair Cheney in the News Again." Urbana, IL: National Council of Teachers of English (June 1995): 12.

Council Chronicle. "Members Angered by Bennett's Critique of NEH Seminars for Teachers." Urbana, IL: National Council of Teachers of English (June 1995): 12.

Council Chronicle. "NCTE, IRA Should 'Brace for Battle.'" Urbana, IL: National Council of Teachers of English (April 1995): 1.

Courts, Patrick L. *Literacy and Empowerment: The Meaning Makers.* Westport, CT: Bergin and Garvey, 1991.

Courts, Patrick L., and Kathleen McInerney. *Assessment in Higher Education: Politics, Pedagogy, and Portfolios.* Westport, CT: Praeger, 1993.

Crawford, James. *Bilingual Education: History, Politics, Theory and Practice.* Trenton, NJ: Crane, 1989.

Cummins, Jim. "From Multiculturalism to Anti-Racist Education: An Analysis of Programes and Policies in Ontario." In *Minority Education: From Shame to Struggle.* Eds. T. Skutnab-Kangas and J. Cummins. Philadelphia: Multilingual Matters, 1988.

———. *Empowering Minority Students*. Sacramento: California Association for Bilingual Education, 1989.

Daniels, Harvey A. "Pacesetter English: Let Them Eat Standards." *English Journal* (November 1994): 44–49.

Darder, Antonia. *Culture and Power in the Classroom*. Westport, CT: Bergin and Garvey Press, 1991.

Delpit, Lisa D. "Skills and Other Dilemmas of a Progressive Black Educator." *Harvard Educational Review* 56:4 (November 1986): 379–385.

———. "The Silenced Dialogue: Power and Pedagogy in Educating Other People's Children." *Harvard Educational Review* 58:3 (August 1988): 280–297.

———. "Acquisition of Literate Discourse: Bowing Before the Master?" *Theory Into Practice* XXXI:4 (Autumn 1992): 298–302.

Derrida, Jacques. *Of Grammatology*. Trans. Gayatri Spivak. Baltimore and London: Johns Hopkins Press, 1976.

de Russy, Candace. "Memorandum" titled "A Personal Vision of SUNY's Future" addressed to "Fellow SUNY Trustees and Chancellor." Reprinted in United University Professions *Bulletin* (August 17, 1995): 1–6.

Dooling, D. M., and Paul Jordan-Smith, eds. *I Become Part of It: Sacred Dimensions in Native American Life*. New York: Parabola Books, 1989.

Elbow, Peter. "Ranking, Evaluating, and Liking; Sorting Out Three Forms of Judgment." *College English* 55:2 (February 1992): 187–206.

Field, James C., and David W. Jardine "'Bad Examples' as Interpretive Opportunities: On the Need for Whole Language to Own Its Shadow." *Language Arts* (1994) 71: 258–262.

Fishman, Andrea R. "Becoming Literate: A Lesson from the Amish." In Lunsford: 29–38.

Flanagan, Anna. "Linguist and NCTE Member Walt Wolfram Takes Controversial Stand on Threatened U.S. Dialects."

Council Chronicle. Urbana, IL: National Council of Teachers of English (June 1995): 1, 4–5.

Foucault, Michel. *The Archaeology of Knowledge and The Discourse on Language*. New York: Pantheon, 1972.

———. "The Discourse on Language." In *The Archaeology of Knowledge*. New York: Pantheon, 1972: 215–238.

———. *Power/Knowledge: Selected Interviews and Other Writings 1972–1977*. Ed. Colin Gordon. New York: Pantheon, 1980.

Freire, Paulo. *Pedagogy of the Oppressed*. New York: Seaview, 1971.

———. *Education for Critical Consciousness*. New York: Seabury, 1973.

———. *The Politics of Education: Culture, Power, and Liberation*. South Hadley, MA: Bergin and Garvey, 1985.

Fox, Geoffrey. "Common Language Doesn't Keep People Together." *The Buffalo News* (December 28, 1995): B–3.

Gardner, Howard. *Multiple Intelligences*. New York: Basic Books, 1993.

Gee, James P. *Social Linguistics and Literatus: Ideology in Discourses*. New York: The Falmer Press, 1990.

Goodman, Kenneth S. *Language and Literacy: The Selected Writings of Kenneth S. Goodman*. Ed. and intro. Frederick V. Gollasch. Vol. 1, *Process, Theory, Research*. Vol. 2, *Reading, Language, and the Classroom Teacher*. Boston: Routledge and Kegan Paul, 1982.

———. "Why Whole Language Is Today's Agenda in Education." *Language Arts* (September 1992): 354–363.

Graves, Donald H. *Writing: Teachers and Children at Work*. Portsmouth, NH: Heinemann Educational Books, 1983.

Hall, Stuart. "Ethnicity: Identity and Difference." *Radical America* 23(4) 1991: 9–20.

Halliday, M. A. K. *Learning How to Mean: Exploration in the Development of Language*. London: Edward Arnold, 1975.

———. *Language as Social Semiotic: The Social Interpretation Language and Meaning*. Baltimore, MD: University Park Press, 1978.

Harste, Jerome C., Virginia A. Woodward, and Carolyn Burke. *Language Stories and Literacy Lessons*. Portsmouth, NH: Heinemann Educational Books, 1984.

Heaney, James. "Schools are a Safe Haven from Streets." *The Buffalo News* (March 29, 1995): A-6.

Heath, Shirley Brice. *Ways with Words: Language, Life, and Work in Communities and Classrooms*. New York: Cambridge University Press, 1983.

Heller, Daniel A. "From the Secondary Section: The Problem of Standard English." *English Journal* (September 1995): 17-18.

Hernstein, Richard J., and Charles Murray. *The Bell Curve*. New York: The Free Press, 1994

Hirsch, E.D., Jr., Joseph F. Kett, and James Trefil. *The Dictionary of Cultural Literacy: What Every American Needs to Know*. Boston: Houghton Mifflin, 1987.

hooks, bell. *YEARNING: Race, Gender, and Cultural Politics*. Boston: South End Press, 1990.

———. *Talking Back*. Boston: South End Press, 1989.

Hourigan, Maureen M. *Literacy as Social Exchange: Intersections of Class, Gender, and Culture*. Albany, NY: State University of New York Press, 1994.

Hutchings, Pat, and Ted Marchese. "Watching Assessment: Questions, Stories, Prospects." *Change* (September/October 1990): 10-38.

Jordan, June. *Moving Towards Home: Political Essays*. London: Virago Press, 1989.

———. "Nobody Mean More to Me than You And the Future Life of Willie Jordan." In Jordan: 175-189.

——. "Problems of Language in a Democratic State." In Jordan: 126–134.

Kincheloe, Joe. "Meet Me Behind the Curtain: The Struggle for a Critical Postmodern Action Research." In McLaren and Giarelli: 71–90.

Kincheloe, Joe L., Peter McLaren, and Shirley Steinberg. "Series Editors Foreword." In Macedo: xiii–xvi.

Koch, Kenneth. *Rose, Where Did You Get That Red: Teaching Great Poetry to Children*. New York: Random House, 1973.

——. *Wishes, Lies, and Dreams*. New York: Perennial Library, 1980.

Labov, William. "Stages in the Acquisition of Standard English." In *Social Dialects and Language Learning*. Ed. Roger Shuy. Champaign, IL: National Council of Teachers of English, 1964.

——. *Language in the Inner-City: Studies in the Black English Vernacular*. Philadelphia: University of Pennsylvania Press, 1972.

——. *Sociolinguistic Patterns*. Philadelphia: University of Pennsylvania Press, 1972.

Lacan, Jacques. "Seminar XX." *Encore*. Paris: Editions du Seuil, 1975.

Lakoff, Robin. *Language and Women's Place*. New York: Harper and Row, 1975.

——. *Talking Power: The Politics of Language in Our Lives*. New York: Basic Books, 1990.

Lane, Charles. "The Tainted Sources of 'The Bell Curve.'" *The New York Review* (December 1, 1994): 14–19.

Lankshear, Colin, and Peter L. McLaren. *Critical Literacy: Politics, Praxis, and the Postmodern*. Albany, NY: State University of New York Press, 1993.

Lofty, John S. "Time to Write: Resistance to Literacy in a Maine Fishing Community." In Lunsford, et al.: 39–49.

Lunsford, Andrea A., Helene Moglen, and James Slevin, eds. *The Right to Literacy*. New York: Modern Language Association, 1990.

Macedo, Donaldo. *Literacies of Power: What Americans Are Not Allowed to Know*. San Francisco: Westview Press, 1994.

Malinowitz, Harriet. "The Rhetoric of Empowerment in Writing Programs." In Lunsford, et al.: 152–162.

Marchese, Ted. "The Search for Learning" (Interview with John Abbott). *AAHE Bulletin* (March 1996): 3–6.

Matalene, Carolyn. "Contrastive Rhetoric: An American Writing Teacher in China." *College English* 47:8 (December 1985): 789–808.

McLaren, Peter. *Life in Schools*. New York: Longman, 1989.

McLaren, Peter L., and James M. Giarelli, eds. *Critical Theory and Educational Research*. Albany, NY: State University of New York Press, 1995.

McLaren, Peter L., and James M. Giarelli. "Introduction: Critical Theory and Educational Research." In McLaren and Giarelli: 1–22.

McLeary, Bill. "NCTE/IRA Standards for English Bring Loud Boos, Few Cheers." *Composition Chronicle* (May 1996): 1–5.

McPike, Elizabeth ed. *American Educator: Learning to Read: Schooling's First Mission*. (Summer 1995) American Federation of Teachers: 6.

———. *American Educator: Spring Brings New Life to the Standards Movement*. (Spring 1996) American Federation of Teachers.

Meyer, Mahlon. "Class Politics: Taiwanese, Chinese Students Don't Mix, Even on U.S. Campuses." *Far Eastern Economic Review* (December 1, 1994): 56–58.

Michaels, Sarah. "Hearing the Connections in Children's Oral and Written Discourse." *Journal of Education* 167:1 (1985): 36–56.

Miller, Keith D., and Elizabeth A. Vander Lei. "Collaboration, Collaborative Communities, and Black Folk Culture." In Lunsford, et al.: 50–60.

Moats, Louisa Cook. "The Missing Foundation in Teacher Education." In McPike (Spring 1996): 9, 43–51

Moffett, James. *Teaching the Universe of Discourse.* Boston: Houghton Mifflin, 1968.

———. *Active Voice: A Writing Program Across The Curriculum.* Upper Montclair, NJ: Boynton/Cook, 1981.

———. "Censorship and Spiritual Education." In Lunsford, et al.: 113–119.

Murray, David. *Forked Tongues: Speech, Writing and Representation in North American Indian Texts.* Bloomington: Indiana University Press, 1991.

Myers, I.B., and M. H. McCaulley. *Manual: A Guide to Development and Use of the Myers-Briggs Type Indicator.* Palo Alto, CA: Consulting Psychologists Press, 1985.

Norwood, C.E., ed. *Literacy as Praxis: Culture, Language, and Pedagogy.* Norwood, NJ: Ablex, 1990.

Ogbu, John. *The Next Generation: An Ethnography of Education in an Urban Neighborhood.* New York: Academic Press, 1974.

———. *Minority Education and Caste.* New York: Academic Press, 1978.

———. Variability in Minority School Performance: A Problem in Search of an Explanation." *Anthropology and Education Quarterly* (December 1987): 312–334.

———. "Cultural Diversity and School Experience." In *Literacy as Praxis: Culture, Language, and Pedagogy.* Ed. C. E. Walsh. Norwood, NJ: Ablex, 1990.

Ortiz, Simon J. "Introduction." *Woven Stone.* Tucson: University of Arizona Press, 1992: 3–33.

Penfield, Joyce, and Jacob L. Ornstein-Galicia. *Chicano English: An Ethnic Contact Dialect.* Philadelphia: John Benjamins, 1985.

Petito, Laura Ann. "Modularity and Constraints in Early Lexical Acquisition: Evidence from Children's Early Language and Gesture." In P. Bloom: 95–126.

Pittenger, David J. "The Utility of the Myers-Briggs Type Indicator," *Review of Educational Research* (Winter 1993): 467–488.

Preston, Dennis R. *Sociolinguistics and Second Language Acquisition.* New York: Basil Blackwell, 1989.

Purcell-Gates, Victoria. *Other People's Words: The Cycle of Low Literacy.* Cambridge, MA: Harvard University Press, 1995.

Ramirez, Manuel III. "The Chicano Bilingual, Cultural Democracy and the Multi Cultural Personality in a Diverse Society." In *Form and Function in Chicano English.* Ed. Jacob Ornstein-Galicia. Rowley, MA: Newbury House, 1984: 99–116.

Richter, David H. *Falling into Theory.* Boston: Bedford Books of St. Martin's Press, 1994.

Robinson, James H. "Contrastive Rhetoric and the Revision Process For East Asian Students." Revision of a paper presented at the 27th Annual TESOL Convention in Atlanta, April 1993 and a chapter in *Comparative Discourse: A Broader View of Contrastive Rhetoric*—to be published.

Rose, Mike. *Lives on the Boundary.* New York: Penguin, 1990.

Schlafly, Phyllis. "What's Wrong with Outcome-Based Education?" *AFA Journal* (Nov/Dec 1993): 20–23.

Scollon, Ronald. "Eight Legs and One Elbow: Stance and Structure in Chinese English Compositions." Paper presented at the International Reading Association, Second North

American Conference on Adult and Adolescent Literacy, Banff, March 21, 1991.

Scollon, Ronald, and Suzanne Scollon. *Narrative, Literacy and Face in Interethnic Communication.* Norwood, NJ: Ablex, 1981.

Shaughnessy, Mina P. *Errors and Expectations.* New York: Oxford University Press, 1977.

Shuy, Roger. *Discovering American Dialects.* Champaign, IL: National Council of Teachers of English, 1967.

Smith, Frank. *Understanding Reading: A Psycholinguistic Analysis of Reading and Learning to Read.* 3d ed. New York: Holt, Rinehart and Winston, 1982.

Smitherman, Geneva. *Talking and Testifyin: The Language of Black America.* Boston: Houghton Mifflin, 1977.

———. "'Students' Right to Their Own Language': A Retrospective." *English Journal* (January 1995): 21–27.

Spanos, William V. *The End of Education: Toward Posthumanism.* Minneapolis: University of Minnesota Press, 1993.

Specter, Michael. "World, Wide, Web: 3 English Words." *New York Times* "Week in Review" (April 14, 1996): sec. 4-1, 5.

Standards for the English Language Arts. National Council of Teachers of English/International Reading Association, 1996.

Steinberg, Shirley, Joe L. Kincheloe, and Aaron D. Gresson III. *Measured Lies: The Bell Curve Examined.* New York: St. Martin's Press, 1996.

Sternberg, R.J. *Beyond IQ.* Cambridge, England: Cambridge University Press, 1985.

Stone, Lynda. "Feminist Educational Research and the Issue of Critical Sufficiency." In McLaren and Giarelli: 145–162.

Strickland, Kathleen, and James Strickland. "I Do Whole Language on Fridays." *English Journal* (February 1996): 17–25.

Tchudi, Stephen, and Susan Tchudi. *The Language Arts Handbook*. Portsmouth, NH: Heinemann Educational Books, 1991.

Thomas, Cal. "The Coming Phonics Revolution." *The Buffalo News* (May 30, 1996): B-3.

Tiedt, Pamela L., and Iris M. Tiedt. *Multicultural Teaching: A Handbook of Activities, Information, and Resources*. New York: Allyn and Bacon, 1995.

Toelken, Barre. "Fieldwork Enlightenment." *Parobola* XX:2 (May 1995): 28–39.

Villanueva, Victor, Jr. *Bootstraps: From an American Academic of Color*. Urbana, IL: National Council of Teachers of English, 1993.

Walsh, Catherine E. *Pedagogy and the Struggle for Voice: Issues of Language, Power, and Schooling for Puerto Ricans*. Westport, CT: Bergin and Garvey, 1991.

Ward, Irene. *Literacy, Ideology, and Dialogue: Towards a Dialogic Pedagogy*. Albany, NY: State University of New York, 1994.

Weaver, Constance. *Reading Process and Practice: From Sociolinguistics to Whole Language*. Portsmouth, NH: Heinemann Educational Books, 1994.

Weaver, Glenn. "Benjamin Franklin and the Pennsylvania Germans." In *The Aliens: A History of Ethnic Minorities in America*. Eds. Dinnerstein, Leonard and Frederic Cople Jaher. New York: Appleton-Century-Crofts, 1970: 47–64.

Will, George F. "A Hair-Raising Peek into Education Madhouse." *The Buffalo News* (July 3, 1995): B-3.

Willis, Paul. *Learning to Labour: How Working Class Kids Get Working Class Jobs*. Westmead, England: Gower, 1977.

Witt, Howard. "California Returns to Education Basics, Plans to Bring Back Spelling Books." *The Buffalo News* (May 24, 1995): A-10.

Wolfram, Walt, and Ralph W. Fasold. *The Study of Social Dialects in American English*. Englewood Cliffs, NJ: Prentice Hall, 1974.

Wolfram, Walt. "Varieties of American English." In *Language in the USA*. Eds. Charles A. Ferguson and Shirley Brice Heath. New York: Cambridge University Press, 1981.

Wordsworth, William. "Preface to Lyrical Ballads (1800)." In *William Wordsworth: The Prelude, Selected Poems and Sonnets*. Ed. Carlos Baker. New York: Holt, Rinehart, and Winston, 1948.

Young, Linda W. L. *Crosstalk and Culture in Sino-American Communication*. New York: Cambridge University Press, 1994.

Index

Patrick Courts is a Distinguished Teaching Professor of English at the State University of New York College at Fredonia.